THE PLANER TRUTH

THE PLANER TRUTH:

A Brief History & Guide
to Servicing Vintage Single Surface Roll Feed Planers
(1850-1950)

DANA MARTIN BATORY

ASTRAGAL PRESS
Lakeville, Minnesota

ISBN 13: 978-1-931626-25-5

Published by
THE ASTRAGAL PRESS
An Imprint of Finney Company
8075 215th Street West
Lakeville, Minnesota 55044
www.finneyco.com
www.astragalpress.com

Printed in the United States of America
1 3 5 7 9 10 8 6 4 2

To My Friends:

E. Cameron Brown & Jeff S. McVey,
for all their kind help and encouragement

Table Of Contents

INTRODUCTION ix

CHAPTER 1: A Brief History..1

CHAPTER 2: Typical Planer Construction 11

CHAPTER 3: Safety 64

CHAPTER 4: Planer System 66

CHAPTER 5: Table Adjustment..109

CHAPTER 6: Bed Roll Adjustment 114

CHAPTER 7: infeed Roll Adjustment 117

CHAPTER 8: Chipbreaker Adjustment 120

CHAPTER 9: Pressure Bar Adjustment 122

CHAPTER 10: Outfeed Roll Adjustment...125

CHAPTER 11: Knife Adjustment..127

CHAPTER 12: Troubleshooting 136

CHAPTER 13: Practical Information and Helpful Hints................................142

CHAPTER 14: Routine Maintenance 147

AFTERWORD 149

INDEX..150

INTRODUCTION

The planer, or surfacer, as it is sometimes called, differs from the jointer in that lumber is fed into it mechanically and dressed to a uniform thickness. For smoothing rough lumber, planing glued-up panels, or reducing the thickness of a board, it is the ideal machine. Unlike other woodworking machines, only one operation can be performed on it, to remove wood from a board, producing a smooth surface parallel with the opposite face.

The planer will not straighten warped or twisted lumber as many think. Even though the pressure of the infeed rolls momentarily flatten a warped board as it moves under the cutterhead, the board will resume its original shape as soon as it leaves the outfeed roll. One face of the warped piece must be planed true or almost true on a jointer. That surface is then placed downward on the table and used to plane the reverse side, before reducing the lumber to the required thickness.

Unfortunately, many of the fine old machines are no longer serviced or else their manufacturers are extinct. Finding an instruction manual is often impossible, which leaves owners in a bit of a fix. For the past 20 years or so, I've owned and operated several planers, ranging from a ca. 1876 24 x 8-inch square-headed John A. White, through a ca. 1950 Buss Machine Works No. 208 20 x 8-inch, to a 1984 Delta RC-33 13 x 6-inch.

My years of tinkering with the machines and a large reference library devoted to vintage woodworking machinery (old catalogs, manuals, etc.) eventually put me into a position where I thought myself comfortable enough to compile a guidebook on single surface, roll feed planers.

I also had the assistance of my brother Todd, a trained mechanic and machinist, who has been the head of several maintenance departments; Jeff McVey, who is not only a service representative of Powermatic and Jet, but an expert at servicing and restoring any old woodworking machine; and Cameron Brown, a woodshop owner and machinery enthusiast of long-standing. Each not only contributed information but proofread the manuscript as well.

This manual purposely deals in generalities since it is aimed at giving the average owner of a vintage planer an informed starting place in setting up his machine and troubleshooting problems that may arise. You will not find highly detailed instructions for servicing particular machines.

There are planers out there that have endured almost 200 years of use and abuse. Before putting a planer, or any old woodworking machine for that matter, back into operation, have it checked out by a professional for wear and damage. *Do not* attempt to run it until those defects have been properly corrected.

Vintage machines are notorious for having been made without guards or with poorly designed ones. Give serious thought to having proper guards made and installed. Shavings hoods in particular, seem very prone to having been removed and lost, probably to speed up access to the cutterhead and its knives.

The forces and vibrations involved in planing are considerable and with continued use, one or more of the parts will eventually get out of alignment. This guide concerns itself only with the adjustment and maintenance of planers, not operation or repairs. If you're unfamiliar with how to operate a planer, consult one of the many fine modern woodworking books at your library, or better yet, buy one for ready reference.

Since they were designed to mechanically dress wood to a uniform thickness, all planers basically share the same features. However, the methods of adjusting the machine for proper operation, varying planing requirements, and compensation for wear, differ from manufacturer to manufacturer. Luckily, there are limited ways of doing so and modern day planers actually vary little from their ancestors in this regard. I occasionally describe the adjustment of selected modern planers only to help in understanding similar vintage models. Familiarizing yourself with any planer manuals you can obtain will be of wonderful help.

Planers are low tech. If you take the time to first examine the mechanics of your machine and each part of its feeding system before attempting any adjustments, you will find things a lot easier. Another good thing to remember is: *If it ain't broke, don't fix it!* In your attempt to fine-tune a planer, you may never achieve the accuracy it already possesses.

Chapter 1

A BRIEF HISTORY

American planing machines were chiefly constructed after two models, the Woodworth (Figs. 1-1 & 1-2) and the Daniels (Figs. 1-3 & 1-4), though each was modified or combined according to the requirements or nature of work.

Both replaced the earlier fixed-knife machines. These were like large hand planes except for the addition of a power-driven feed system which moved the work past a stationary knife or bit.

The more familiar Woodworth planers, with their roll-feed or lag-bed (endless bed) systems, belong to a class called *parallel* planers.

In 1828, William Woodworth was issued a patent for a machine combining a rotary cutterhead with rolls to hold the lumber against the force of the knives and to hold the lumber down to the bed so the lumber was reduced to an even thickness. Initially, the wood was fed through the planer by a rack and pinion system.

The Daniels, or traverse planing machine, also called a dimension, traveling carriage, or reciprocating planer, was ideally suited to dressing twisted and warped lumber. It was patented in 1834 by Thomas E. Daniels. Here the bed or carriage moved back and forth like the bed of the metal planer used in machine shops. It was used chiefly in the heaviest railway or wagon work.

Dimension planers were made as late as World War II by Stetson-Ross Co. and L. Power & Co. for building wooden mine sweepers.

The author knows of no Daniels planing machine or dimension planer still in commercial operation. If you know of one, please contact me. However, complete Daniels planers made by Richardson, Meriam & Co., exactly like the one in the 1856 Fay & Co. catalog, are on display at the Slater Mill Historic Site, Pawtucket, RI, and the Percy & Small Shipyard at the Maine Maritime Museum, and there is a J.A. Fay & Co. model at the Smithsonian.

Dimension planers did not use rolls to move the work piece past the cutterhead; instead, the lumber was dogged to a long table running on planed true cast-iron ways. The table was made to travel backwards and forwards under the cutters by a rack and pinion gear or other gearing. Actually, machines constructed with a traveling table are the only true planing machines.

On the Daniels planer, a horizontal arm (Fig. 1-5) fitted with a cutter at either end revolved over the board or timber as it passed beneath. This method of removing material is called fly cutting. The cutters worked the wood at right angles to the grain and during both traverses of the table. The passage of the lumber under the cutters generated a true planed surface on top parallel to that of the ways. This one surface could then be used as a base plane for working out the other three surfaces in rectangular work.

These were once the only class of planing machines that would take lumber out of twist or warp, making it perfectly true and ready for gluing up as it left the machine. With this machine any kind, size, or condition of material could be worked. When very thin lumber had to be planed, weights or pressure rolls were used.

In the typical Daniels planer the arm was supported in a sash-frame adjustable vertically by a screw for varying thicknesses of work. A cast-iron disk, known as the 'dead-weight,' usually hung concentric with the cutters and kept the lumber down when thin, and acted also as a sort of chip-breaker. A pressure-roll turned in a frame in front of the cutters.

The bed of the Daniels planer had to be more than twice the length of the table, and the latter had to be longer than the longest piece the machine was ever expected to accommodate. The great bed length made the machine very bulky and convinced many manufacturers to continue to make the framing all of wood. One or two used iron uprights on the frame bolted to a wooden bed. There were objections to this, since the wooden parts yielded to atmospheric influences while the iron did not, and the quality of their work was affected. Later high-grade machines had metal framing, although their relative expense prevented their extensive use (Fig. 1-6).

While the transverse action of the cutters in a Daniels planer did not distort the lumber being trued, their action was very slow. To remedy this, the rotary cutterhead of the Woodworth planer was soon fitted parallel to the traversing bed of the Daniels (Figs. 1-7 & 1-8). It was adjustable by screws for varying thicknesses and carried its own spring-pressure bars or rolls.

Such a machine would plane true and twisted lumber as well as the old, and had great advantages in the long life of the cutting-edges compared to those of the Daniels, and in the rapid feed. Other machines incorporated both types and featured an attachment of feeding-rolls for the use of the machine on the pure Woodworth principle. The carriage was locked stationary and the lumber fed over it as in the typical machine. The switch from a Daniels planer to a Woodworth planer was made very simple and easy.

The comparatively slow feed of the Daniels caused its slower development than the parallel classes of planers. While the earlier speeds of less than 20 fpm were later much exceeded, the limited capacity of the machine restricted its use to shops handling larger and heavier sizes of lumber for car, bridge, or other engineering purposes.

On some Daniels planers, the cutterhead was set at an angle, producing a shear cut and eliminating to some extent the tearing of cross-grained wood.

The validity of the Woodworth patent was contested for many years. One part of the patent, the roller-feed arrangement, was known in Great Britain years before, a patent having been granted in 1811. After several controversial renewals, the Woodworth patent finally expired in 1865.

Eventually, feed rolls were not relied upon to hold the work to the table. A chipbreaker was added immediately before the cutterhead and a pressure bar after it to improve the quality of the planing.

The early single surfacers, "pony planers" in American literature, "thicknessers" in England, with rise and fall beds, were built under Woodworth's patents to meet the need for a machine that could be rapidly adjustable in miscellaneous shops. The bearings of the upper cutterhead were fixed and the rolls had only rubber adjustment (Fig. 1-9), if any at all. The variation for thickness was usually obtained by raising and lowering the table by a crank or handwheel. The separate adjustment of the series of rolls was thus entirely avoided, the machine became much shorter and more compact, and a stiffness and solidity was obtained for the upper cutters which widely popularized the system.

Cutterhead speeds on these early belt-driven machines ran at about 4000 rpm, which was the maximum that could be obtained with belt drives.

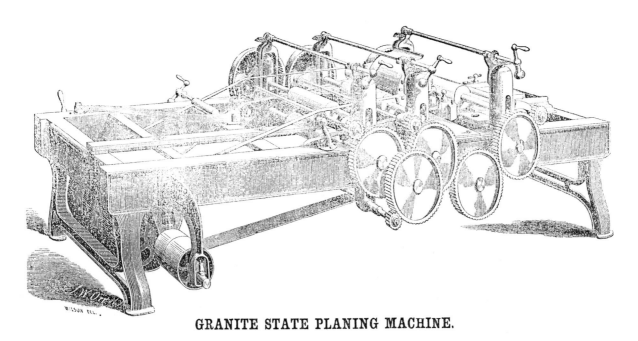

GRANITE STATE PLANING MACHINE.

Fig. 1-1: Granite State Planing Machine. Improved Planing, Tongueing, And Grooving Machine. Woodworth Type. J.A. Fay & Co., 1856 Catalog.

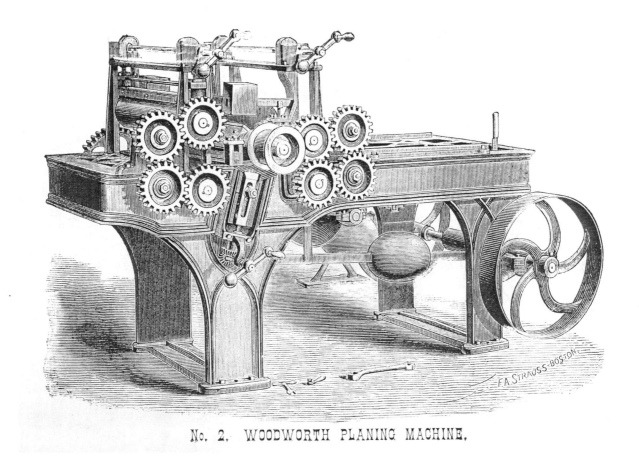

No. 2. WOODWORTH PLANING MACHINE.

Fig. 1-2: No. 2 Woodworth Planing Machine. Richardson, Meriam & Co., 1867 Catalog.

DANIELS'S
IMPROVED PLANING MACHINE,
WITH REED'S FEED MOTION.

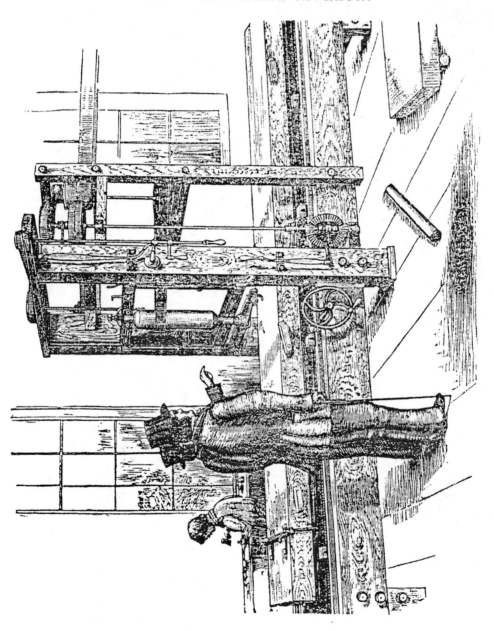

Fig. 1-3: Daniels's Improved Planing Machine. J.A. Fay & Co., 1856 Catalog.

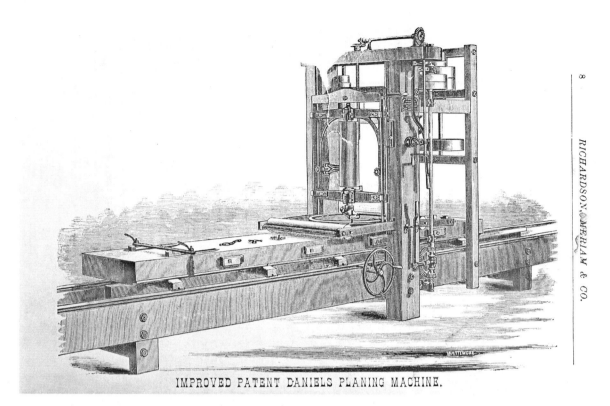

Fig. 1-4: Improved Patent Daniels Planing Machine. Richardson, Meriam & Co., 1867 Catalog.

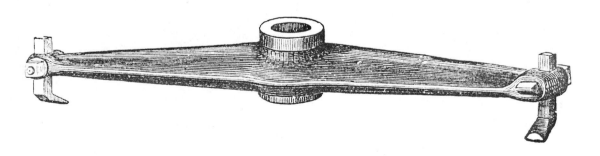

Fig. 1-5: Improved Patent Daniels' Planing Arm. Richardson, Meriam & Co., 1867 Catalog.

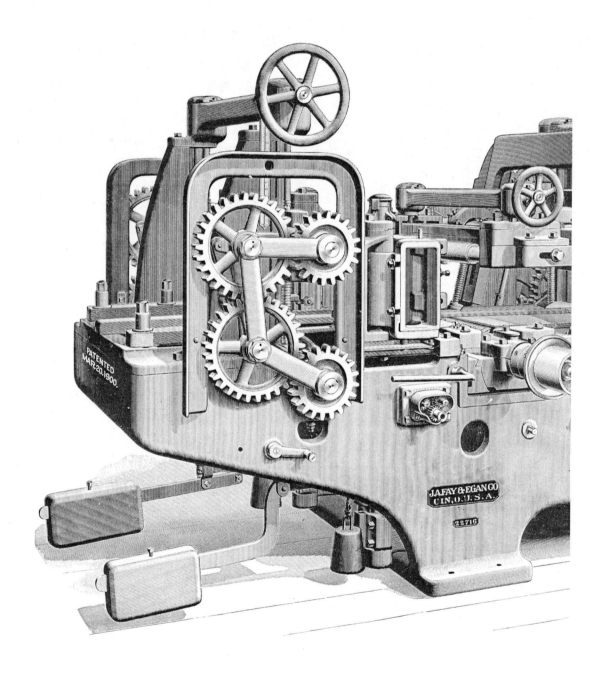

Fig. 1-6: No. 32 Improved Iron-Frame Dimension Planing Machine. Daniels Type. J.A. Fay & Egan Co., Catalogue Series L Circa 1901.

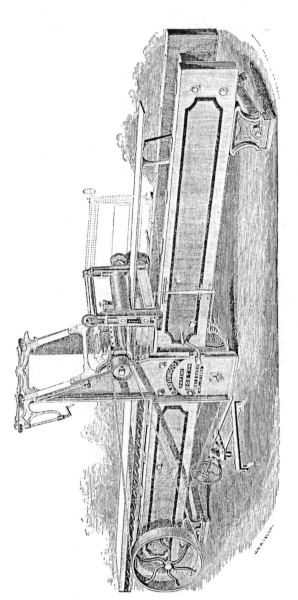

"Gray & Woods" Improved Patent Combination Planer.

COMMON SIZE, TO PLANE AND DOG OUT OF WIND, WITH CARRIAGE.

TO PLANE 24 INCHES WIDE AND FROM 8 FEET LONG UPWARDS, AS ORDERED.

THIS machine is too widely and favorably known to require an extended description in this place, but we have recently greatly improved the general construction, and introduced many valuable and important features, and shall be pleased to furnish to those who may desire, a circular sheet in which these improvements are fully described.

The above cut is not a correct representation of our Common size as now constructed, our present machine being built from

an entirely new set of patterns throughout, similar in style to the Extra Heavy size, represented on page 26. The above, however, shows the manner in which the Feed-Roll attachment is used for surfacing boards, and some details not shown in cut of Extra Heavy size.

The receiving pulley on the Common size is 14 by 6 inches, and should make 630 revolutions per minute. The belting required for this size is as follows: for cylinder, $17\frac{10}{12}$ feet of 4-inch; for feed-works, $26\frac{6}{12}$ feet of 3-inch, and $23\frac{4}{12}$ feet of $2\frac{1}{2}$-inch.

Fig. 1-7: Improved Patent Combination Planer. Daniels & Woodworth Type. Patent Re-issued Apr. 17, 1860. S.A. Woods Machine Co., June 1, 1876 Catalog.

J. A. FAY & CO'S
NEW AND IMPROVED DIMENSION PLANER.

Fig. 1-8: New And Improved Dimension Planer. Combination Of The Traversing Carriage Of The Daniels' Planer With The Cutterhead Of The Woodworth Planing Machine. J.A. Fay & Co., 1856 Catalog.

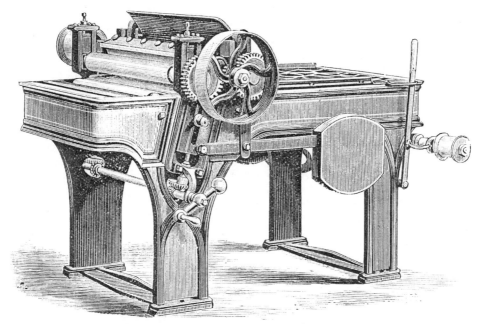

No. 0. SMALL CYLINDER PLANING MACHINE.

Fig. 1-9: No. 0 Small Cylinder Planing Machine. Richardson, Meriam & Co., 1867 Catalog. The top two feed rolls and the two knife, wrought iron cutterhead are connected in one slide so the crank raises and lowers them together at an angle with the driving shaft keeping the belts tight at all times. The feeds rolls could be fitted with rubber springs or with weights and rubber springs combined.

Fig. 1-10: John A. White Co. 24 x 8 Planer. Circa 1876. Author's Collection.

Fig. 1-11: No. 208 Planer. 20 x 8. Buss Machine Works. Circa 1950. Author's Collection.

Chapter 2

TYPICAL PLANER CONSTRUCTION

FRAME

A planer must be ruggedly built to take the shock and stress of cutting wide lumber. It has a very heavy and rigid base or frame which is often bolted to the floor. In the case of planers like Defiance Machine Works' 26" Patent Four Roll Single Surface Planer Frame (Fig. 2-1), the massive casting was of sufficient weight (7000 lb.) to stay in place without fastening it to the floor. Its bottom was planed true so the machine would have a uniform bearing on the floor.

The earliest planers had frames of mortised and tenoned hardwood timbers bolted together (Fig. 2-2), which were gradually replaced with cast iron beginning about 1850.

The newer style frames often had two cast-iron side panels that extended down to the floor (Fig. 2-3). These were keyed, doweled, and bolted together with heavy cross panels and/or girts. Due to the lack of a one-piece base, these old-style planers had to be kept leveled and shimmed or the side frames would sag to the contour of the floor beneath it. This resulted in the operator having to have arms like Hercules to crank the table up and down and cutterhead bearing misalignment problems.

S. A. Woods Machine Co. as early as 1876 was planing the frames of their machines (Fig. 2-4) all assembled, a method which gave greater stability and firmness to the machine, a method not customary with other makers.

The use of cast-iron frames was spurred by an English innovation. About 1862 Henry Wilson (then manager of the firm of Powis, James, and Co., London) developed the box or hollow core frame. Instead of frames being bolted together in pieces, they were cast in one solid mass around a sand core which was later removed, thus securing greater rigidity, enabling saws and cutterheads to be driven at high speeds without vibration. This was unattainable in machines made with light iron or wooden framing.

By the mid-1860s American woodworking machinery manufacturers began to slowly replace the clumsy and weak wooden frames and girded cast-iron panels with the recently popularized hollow core, cast-iron frames and bases.

The models had one-piece hollow core cast-iron bases with wide flanges planed on the bottom to give the machine a firm, even bearing on the floor (Fig. 2-5). A one-piece frame will stay in alignment under the most grueling conditions.

Crescent Machine Co.'s 1912 30 x 6-inch Variable Speed Planer (Fig. 2-6) was unique in combining several elements.

The frame was made in three parts, a base and two side panels. The base was pyramidal in general shape with heavy ribs running crosswise on the underside from corner to corner, making it impossible to spring or twist under any ordinary conditions. The sides were rigidly bolted to the base on planed-off surfaces. Taper-pin dowels were used to keep them in exact position. The panels were cored-out hollow, to give extreme stiffness.

Usually in planers of this size the panels (not cored hollow) rested directly on the floor and were connected by cross pieces bolted between. When such a machine was set on a floor that was slightly uneven, a twisting strain was thrown onto the working parts of the machine, or the machine could be racked out of alignment in shipping or handling.

But this could not occur with this form of construction, since the entire machine was supported on a single casting—the base, and the base so shaped that all shocks and strains were absorbed. No amount of jarring in shipping or handling could possibly throw the machine out of alignment.

Subsequent improvements to planers were in the direction of greater strength and stiffness of the bed and frame, more ample bearing and wearing surfaces, and the more frequent use of steel.

Typically, the heavy table or bed consists of one solid iron casting heavy ribbed under the cutterhead with long and wide bearing surfaces, but on some larger machines it is made in several parts fastened to a cast-iron frame. They are precisely machined and finished and, in the best machines, hardened to resist wear. A ledge is usually milled or fastened to the table sides to hold the lumber within the limits of the knives. The bed moves up or down between the sides of the frame.

Many older machines have a false table directly below the cutterhead which could be taken out and reground when worn hollow by the downward pressure of the cutterhead knives (Fig. 2-7). Others had a strip of steel let into the table at that point. Oliver Machinery Co.'s 1949 No. 361 Single Surface Planer (Fig. 2-8) had a center table of cast chrome alloy steel, making it very hard. The author's Buss No. 208 has a chromium-plated table.

Baxter D. Whitney Co. used tables of extra thickness, strongly ribbed and accurately machined. The center table (Fig. 2-9) under the cutterhead was chilled (hardened) to prevent wear and to eliminate the necessity of frequently dressing it over. It had a ground surface and presented a glass-hard, wear-resisting surface.

On some of the oldest planers, the front and rear tables have open slots or diamonds or ornate cutouts in them to allow dust and shavings to fall through (Fig. 2-10).

Greenlee Brothers & Co.'s ca. 1944 No. 110 Six-Roll Single Planer (Fig. 2-11) was unique in having the infeed table mounted on springs so the lumber could equalize between the top and bottom rolls, permitting it to enter with no extra effort on the part of the operator, even on heavy cuts. The outfeed table had independent screw vertical adjustment on its outer end to support long or heavy stock.

Some planers like Boice-Crane Co.'s 1935 Little Giant (Fig. 2-12) were built around a very heavy, one-piece U frame of cast iron. Their frame supported and maintained constant alignment of the cutterhead's S-K-F ball bearings and the four bearings of the two power feed rolls and also kept the vertical table ways to a constant, snug, but free sliding fit. By avoiding a frame of pieces bolted together, it could never shift out of alignment under the most relentless heavy cut.

H. B. Smith Machine Co.'s 1902 No. 30-A Cabinet Surfacer (Fig. 2-13) had a limiting bar across the machine to prevent the possibility of getting too heavy a cut for the cutterhead.

THICKNESS ADJUSTMENT

There are two ways of adjusting a planer for various thicknesses: the bed may rise or fall (Fig. 2-14) or the cutterhead will raise or lower (Fig. 2-15). The former design seems to have always predominated because of its simplicity, particularly in belting up the machine.

In those machines where the cutterhead was designed to adjust vertically, the bearings and cutterhead moved up and down and were clamped in planed tracks or ways. This adjustment was by screws geared together by a shaft across the bed with bevel gears.

The bed on J. A. Fay & Co.'s three knife, double-belted Granite State Improved Planing, Tongueing, And Grooving Machine (Fig. 1-1) remained stationary while the cutterhead and feed rolls were all individually adjusted for different thicknesses, a bit impractical. Richardson, Meriam & Co.'s 1867 No. 2 Woodworth Planer (Fig. 1-2) was adjusted the same way. C. B. Rogers & Co. was still using this awkward setup on its 1888 No. 7 and No. 8 Planers (Figs. 2-16 & 2-17).

Many early builders were content to depend upon the screws and the fit of the slides to keep the cutterhead true and the bearing boxes in line and free from binding, but better quality machines used a one-piece cast-iron yoke or cross-girt to rigidly support them (Fig. 2-18).

Oliver Machinery Co.'s ca. 1948 No. 299 Single Surfacer (Fig. 2-19) had a one-piece casting located over the base casting. Both upper rolls, the chipbreaker, the pressure bar, the cutterhead, and the cutterhead motor were located in this casting, or yoke. Perfect and permanent alignment of these parts was insured. Bentel & Margedant Co.'s ca. 1890 No. 41 Monitor Surface Planer (Fig. 2-20) had a similar design.

There are two methods of raising or lowering the table: one is by wedges (Fig. 2-21) and the other by screws (Fig. 2-22).

The most common mechanism is still the screw type. In this form, two heavy Acme screws extend from the base to the lower part of the planer bed, one on each side. These are connected by shaft and gears to a large handwheel which operates them in unison and gives an up-and-down movement to the bed, which slides in vertical ways. The screw movement is sometimes considered inferior to the wedge movement, because on early machines there was a tendency of the whole bed to tip forward when a board entered the machine, and backward when it left the machine.

To avoid this, some manufacturers used two pair of screws. Defiance Machine Works' 26" Patent Four Roll Single Surface Planer (Fig. 2-1) had its table supported on four heavy steel screws and fitted to the inside of the frame in broad guide ways on either side. It was raised and lowered by power with a slight movement of a convenient hand lever. An ingenious device automatically arrested the movement of the table at its extreme up or down movements, preventing any possible chance of jamming the table when going up or down to its full limit.

Some builders got around the problem another way. The table on American Saw Mill Machinery Co.'s 1919 "Jewel" Planer (Fig. 2-23) was a single casting, deep, strong, heavily ribbed, and gibbed to the outer edges of the main frame, to which it could be securely locked at any point,

thus avoiding all rocking or vibration. Rowley & Hermance Co.'s 1898 "Peacemaker" Double Belted Single Surfacer's table could likewise be quickly and securely clamped to the frame, making it as solid as the frame itself (Fig. 2-24).

The author's John A. White planer is an unusual screw type. The planer has one massive steel pillar or column centered directly under the bed which slides up and down within the hollow cast-iron base. A large gear on the pillar is revolved by another gear on the handwheel shaft. The pillar gear drives two smaller gears which turn the two large vertical screws, raising or lowering the bed. The bed is stabilized by both the pillar and the screws to prevent rocking. The tangent double gearing also acts as a clamp.

The cutterhead, rolls, chipbreaker, and pressure bar on several modern planers are guided by four columns and raised or lowered as a unit on four screws, one located in each corner, connected by a chain and sprockets. So far I have yet to find such a design on any vintage planers. If you know of any, please tell me.

The inclined plane or wedge type is used on the best and most expensive planers. It is the most rigid and precise, supposedly accurate to within .0001 of an inch. The design probably originated with Baxter D. Whitney.

Whitney built his first planer in 1846 (Fig. 2-25). In 1866 he invented a new type, displayed at the 1867 Paris Exposition, where it received a silver medal and became known as the "Silver Medal Planer" (Fig. 2-26). This supplanted the company's first planer. Designed into this Silver Medal Planer were such features as the upper and lower wedges for support and adjustment of the bed (Fig. 2-27), still standard in all heavy planers now in production, thus proving the soundness of the original design (Figs. 2-28 & 2-29).

The wedge movement consists of two pairs of cast-iron wedges. On production machines like Frank H. Clement Co.'s No. 4 (Fig. 2-21) the bed was planed the whole length and was raised and lowered on heavy, well-fitted inclines, the lower or movable ones sliding on tracks cast upon the framing. All these surfaces were carefully hand-scraped to a precision fit.

The table is bolted to the upper pair, which rests on top of the lower pair. These are moved in and out by a screw worked by a large handwheel. This movement of the lower wedges raises or lowers the upper wedges and thereby the table. The lower wedges slide in horizontal guides or ways, the upper wedges in vertical ways.

On the Frank H. Clement No. 4 the lower incline was moved by two heavy square threaded screws working together by cut gears and operated by a large central handwheel. One revolution of the wheel gave 1/32" vertical motion to the bed.

On the larger and heavier machines, the table can be raised or lowered by a motor-driven hoist.

One planer built by the Oliver Machinery Co. had a small handwheel in front that allowed the bed to be raised or lowered fractionally without using the larger handwheel.

Some planers like H. B. Smith Machine Co.'s No. 30-A Cabinet Surfacer (Fig. 2-13) had a power and hand hoist equipped to automatically throw out when the bed had been raised to within 1/8" of the cutterhead. Likewise, Boice-Crane Co.'s hand raised 1935 "Little Giant" (2-12) had a safety stop that prevented the table from ever striking the knives.

FEED MECHANISMS

Planers may be of two kinds, roll-feed (Fig. 2-30) or continuous traveling bed (Fig. 2-31). In the first, the most common type, the bed remains stationary while the lumber passes over it driven by geared feed rolls. In the second, an endless bed or conveyor belt, travels under the revolving cutterhead, carrying the lumber with it. The larger planers were of the first class, while many small ones in the 1880s and 1890s were built with the traveling bed.

These lag-beds planers, sometimes known as Farrar planers, are named after James Farrar who invented the machine around 1855. Also known as mill planers in the western United States, they were intended for heavy and rapid surfacing and well suited for wet or icy lumber upon which the Woodworth rolls might slip. The weight of the

work favored the feed, instead of resisting it. They had a speed of about 60 fpm and in their 'pony' form were very popular in the United States, even displacing other forms in certain classes of work. They were generally used when a high-quality surface finish was not needed.

The bed usually consisted of a series of cast-iron slats or bars flexibly connected together powered by gear driven rolls at either end of the machine. It past under the cutterhead, and the bearing surfaces over which it slid were usually made of chilled iron for hardness and ground smooth. Pressure rolls kept the timber firmly on the bed. Though the machines had a rapid and powerful feed, they required considerable care in manufacture and maintenance. The heavy friction to which they were subjected, unless carefully guarded against, caused early deterioration.

The popular roll-feed planers, which this book deals with, were far more simple and easier to manufacture and maintain.

On the smaller and/or cheaper planers only the upper rolls were power driven (Fig. 2-32); the larger, better quality machines used expansion gearing so all the rolls could be power driven (Fig. 2-33).

The bed rolls were solid, milled from steel bar stock or forged of steel. Baxter D. Whitney & Son's 1930 No. 37 Heavy Duty Single Planer had its feed rolls made of fine grain iron cast on through steel shafts.

On Greenlee's No. 110 Six-Roll Single Planer (Fig. 2-11) the bottom rolls and the top outfeed roll were of iron cast to heavy steel shafts in such a manner that they could never come loose. The materials of construction resisted bending stresses, and the rolls and shaft ends were accurately ground.

The simplest form of drive was a belt from the cutterhead to a shaft, which through a series of gears or belts and pulleys, was connected to the feed rolls (Fig. 2-34). A feed driven directly from the cutterhead always maintains the proper feed proportion, regardless of any belt slippage. The feed increases or diminishes in proportion to the speed of the cutterhead. If the cutterhead is slowed down, say by a heavy cut or hardwood, the feed also automatically slows down. On some machines the feed rolls were chain driven (Fig. 2-35). On better machines the feed rolls were geared at both ends so there was equal pressure on the lumber for its whole length (Fig. 2-36).

Gears machine-molded from cut patterns and faced off on their sides were considered by some manufacturers to be better than cut gears, as they could last 30% longer. This was due to the fact that all cast iron is harder on the immediate surface than on the inside, and it is this surface chill that gives the wearing qualities to a gear. However, gears cut from the solid seem to have been the standard practice. It was believed they produced a uniform and steady movement to the feed, free from backlash or chatter as with ordinary cast gearing, consequently, smooth and perfect planing could be secured. Some manufacturers used both, cut gears for high speed use and molded gears for low speed.

The gears on some 1940s Fay & Egan planers were cut from solid semi-steel, the teeth meshing perfectly, giving a smooth, practically silent, and power-saving drive. This type was supposed to eliminate the crunching, grinding, and expensive breakage caused by a cast-iron gear drive.

For well over a hundred years planers got their power from a countershaft belt driven by a main shaft, which in turn was powered by a waterwheel or steam engine.

Early production planers were double belted (Fig. 2-37) thereby equally dividing the strain and diminishing the wear on the bearings. Power was transmitted to the cutterhead by flat belts to a pulley on each end instead of driving it from only one end as in the case of the jointers. Some cheaper makes of single surfacers were single belted (Fig. 2-38).

When gears were used only on one end of the feed-rolls, a lifting action was produced which had a tendency to feed the board through obliquely. Many builders like S. A. Woods Machine Co. avoided this difficulty by gearing the feed-rolls at both ends, causing an equal pressure on both edges of the board, and feeding it through straight (Fig. 2-39). The gears also wore evenly and were more than twice as durable.

Most planers were equipped with step pulleys or other mechanisms such as a clutch or friction feed that enabled the operator to vary the rate of feed (Fig. 2-40).

Crescent Machine Co.'s 1910 No. 218 Planer (Fig. 2-41) was provided with a new variable friction feed, driven directly from cutterhead by belt. Any speed from 12 to 50 fpm was instantly available by simply turning a handwheel. The changes could be made even while the machine was in motion. A pointer and scale indicated the feed. A throw-off lever, at the side of the table, could be used for instantly stopping the feed, without stopping the machine. The variable speed mechanism utilized the fact that the surface of a spinning disk progressively revolves faster as you move outward from its center (Fig. 2-42). A handwheel moved a revolving friction disk keyed to a drive shaft to the feed rolls, up and down against a spinning disk.

Smoothness of cut, other things being equal, depends upon the speed of the feed rolls. Feeds, like cutterhead speeds and machine sizes, depended upon the particular make of machine. With a cutterhead speed of 5,000 rpm, a machine could have feeds of 16, 21, 27, and 33 fpm, or more. Cheaper machines had fewer variations in feed, possibly only one. As a rule this was about 24 fpm for a cutterhead speed of 4,500 rpm. On better models it was possible to adjust for speeds. The ordinary range was from 15 to 30 fpm depending upon the size and make of the machine. Special high-speed machines could run soft woods as fast as 75 fpm. If the machine was a good one and was properly adjusted, it could plane lumber as thin as 1/16".

The belt and gears that drove the feed rolls were entirely separate from the belt powering the cutterhead. This was so the feed rolls could be stopped instantly in case of accident, since the momentum of the rapidly revolving cutterhead would keep it running for perhaps a minute after the power was shut off. Also, if the cut was too heavy and the machine slowed down, the feed could be shut off until full speed was regained. The feed was controlled by a lever at the front of the machine which engaged or disengaged the rolls at the will of the operator. On the author's White planer it is a simple idler pulley with a hand hold which is pulled back manually to slacken the feed belt tension.

Equipping planers with electric motor drives dates to about 1904 (Fig. 2-43). On small planers, the feed mechanism was driven by the same motor as the cutterhead, but on larger machines, designers soon saw the value in having the feed mechanism driven by an independent motor (Fig. 2-44). However, some early belt driven planers did have the belts and gears driving the feed rolls entirely separate from the cutterhead drive. The rates of feed varied considerably from machine to machine from as low as 10 fpm to as high as 150 fpm. These newer machines were also equipped with better safety devices for stopping the feeding mechanism.

On some more advanced planers a speed control was also available for changing the rpm of the cutterhead (Fig. 2-45).

Most modern planers are driven by a motor mounted directly on the shaft on which the cutterhead is mounted. This was a great advantage since it eliminated long drive belts, making the machine more compact and easier to maintain and there was also less oiling and fewer belts to adjust. It is more efficient since loss of motion through belt slippage is eliminated. However, it does mean that if the motor goes bad you have no recourse but to get it repaired. There is no such thing as simply buying a new motor and belting it up. It also confines cutterhead speed to 3600 rpm, unless one has recourse to frequency changers.

Guards for gears, cutterheads, etc., on the early machines were usually inadequate and more often than not, non-existent (Fig. 2-46). Safety really didn't become a concern until around 1917 when an influx of unskilled operators poured into factories to meet war production. On modern machines the entire feeding mechanism is completely guarded or enclosed in the side castings (Fig. 2-47). The feed rolls as well as all the gear wheels run in roller or ball bearings.

CUTTERHEADS

Cutterheads differ in shape and in the number of knives mounted on them. Some heads are triangular (Fig. 2-48) and have three knives; others are square (Figs. 2-49 & 2-50) and equipped with either two or four knives; still others are round (Fig. 2-51) with two to six knives. The use of the round safety cutterhead dates to 1908 in the United States. The speed of cutterheads can vary from 3600 to 5000 rpm.

Cutterheads were made of wrought iron, crucible steel (cast steel), and tool steel, and could be forged, cast, or turned to shape from bar steel. Forging was the most favored method.

Wrought iron is the purest form of the metal containing only a very small amount of other elements but containing 1-3% by weight of slag (oxidized impurities) in the form of particles elongated in one direction, giving the iron a characteristic grain. It is more rust-resistant than steel and welds more easily and was used for chains, hooks, bars, etc.

Early cutterheads were made of wrought iron no doubt because of its economy in production. Richardson, Meriam & Co.'s No. 2 Woodworth (Fig. 1-2), had wrought iron cutterheads. S. A. Woods Machine Co. was still using them as late as 1876.

Crucible steel is made by melting accurately proportioned mixtures of wrought iron (and/or steel scrap), charcoal, and alloying elements (such as silicon, manganese, chromium, molybdenum, and vanadium) in covered crucibles which hold 50 to 100 lb. of metal. This is the oldest and simplest method for producing steel in a molten condition, hence called cast steel.

The high quality which can be obtained in crucible steel is due to the control of the composition and the temperature of the metal in the process, as well as to freedom from the influence of oxidizing gases. This steel is particularly suited to the production of small castings requiring special physical properties such as tool steels. Crucible steel appears to have been the metal of choice for cutterheads.

Tool steels are usually quenched and tempered, to obtain the required properties. Since forged tool steel has a more even temper than cheaper grades of steel a cutterhead of smaller cross section could be used without danger of springing out of true. Its use was sporadic.

In the 1930s Baxter D. Whitney & Son still offered square cutterheads made from heat-treated tool steel forgings uniform in quality and temper. To prolong the life of the cutterheads and secure chipbreaker lips that would resist wear, as well as furnish a uniform bearing for the knives, hardened steel strips were inserted in the cutterheads after which they were machined to the correct shape. The cutterheads would carry two or four knives (Fig. 2-52).

Greenlee Brothers & Co.'s No. 110 Six-Roll Single Planer had a cutterhead machined from a solid forged blank of high-grade steel (Fig. 2-53). Great care was taken in the heat treatment to secure a maximum of toughness and resistance to the stresses it had to withstand. After forging, the head was rough turned and then allowed to season. The seasoning was repeated after other machining operations to ensure a head that would 'stay put' at all times.

Steel is the third of the chief forms of iron, and is in composition a connecting link between cast iron and wrought iron. While resembling cast iron in containing carbon, it differs from it in being a carefully purified, malleable iron, to which a definite proportion of carbon has subsequently been added, the amount varying from .20–1%, depending on the desired mechanical properties.

In casting, an object is formed to the shape required by pouring the molten metal into a mold, as distinct from one shaped by working. I have yet to discover a truly one-piece cast cutterhead in any of the literature.

In forging, an object is made from hot, softened metals shaped to form by heavy hammers or heavy presses. By being beaten into their rough shapes, they are made extremely hard and strong. Cutterheads were usually made from one-piece solid forgings machined to their final shapes.

The knives in older machines are bolted to flat surfaces milled on a square block. Slots in the knives (Fig. 2-54) not only allowed them to be fastened to the block but also allowed for adjustment as the knives were ground narrower.

Usually cutterheads carried either three or four knives. The flats for the knives were shaped so as to act as a cap or chipbreaker. The cutterheads were usually made of forged steel, all in one piece. American Saw Mill Machinery Co.'s "Jewel" planer (Fig. 2-23) had a square cutterhead made from high grade forged steel, accurately milled and balanced with lips projecting under the cutting edge of the two knives to strengthen them and to ensure smooth work.

Very good results were also obtained by the use of wrought-iron bodies, into which the spindles were forced or shrunk, and one builder cast the body around the spindle, using a so-called welding compound to effect the joint.

The planing of T-slots in the faces of the cutterheads for the heads of the knife-bolts was the best practice. Many builders planed slots in two sides and had the other sides with tapped holes only. Another had lips on two sides and slots on all four sides (Fig. 2-55). Some had no slots, but tapped all holes, others, lipped and slotted on four sides. This required that all knives had to have equally spaced slots to prevent twisted bolts or stripped threads.

S. A. Woods Machine Co. in 1876 was using solid square wrought iron cutterheads, with or without lips, slotted upon two sides for the attachment of special cutters, and tapped upon the two remaining sides for ordinary straight knives.

Square cutterheads with Babbitt bearings ran at 3,000 to 4,000 rpm.

Another advantage with round heads is that they are stiffer than a square head of the same cutting circle because they are of greater sectional area. This makes a steadier running head, with less tendency to vibrate, and which is less liable to get out of balance.

Bentel & Margedant Co.'s ca. 1890s planers, such as the No. 42 Hamilton Surface Planer (Fig. 2-34), featured patented triangular shear-knife cutterheads arranged with three straight knives set at a shearing angle so that cross-grained or knotty timber could be planed with unusual smoothness. The head was milled in such a way that the knives were angled horizontally but still at the same vertical height (Fig. 2-60).

The Norris Patent Improved Diagonal Planer with an optional polishing head, patented May 9, 1871, Mar. 24, 1874, and Mar. 1879, & Sept. 1879 (Fig. 2-56), had its cutterhead placed at an angle of 45° to the feed rolls. This gave a uniform cut on the stiles and rails of doors, sash, and other work having grain running at different angles, insuring a perfectly smooth surface, regardless of knots or gross-grained places in material being worked, without knocking out or splitting the bars and muntins. The wedge bed machine would do 500–600 doors in ten hours.

S. A. Woods Machine Co.'s similar 1876 Improved Door Planer (Fig. 2-57) had its cutterhead set at an angle.

Bentel & Margedant took the idea one step further with their 1890 No. 44 Diagonal Surface Planer (Fig. 2-58) which not only had their standard triangular shear-knife cutterhead, but also had the cutterhead set diagonally. This made the machine especially adapted for very smooth planing of either cross-grained or knotty lumber, or for work joined together crossways or that consisted of various woods with different grains or hardness.

SIZE

The size of a planer is indicated by the width of the table and the length of the knives, and can range from 12"–54" and 4"–8" thick (Figs. 2-59 & 2-60). Small planers, usually less than 18", are often referred to in old literature as "pony" planers because of their size. A good machine will plane lumber as thin as 1/8", or even 1/16".

Bentel & Margedant Co.'s No. 52 60" Power Feed Planer, ca. 1890, was the largest commercial model ever built (Fig. 2-61). It was also offered combined with a 60" jointer and molding heads.

One of the great advantages of wider planers is that material may be safely fed diagonally, giving a shear cut (Figs. 2-62 & 2-63). This is of great help when surfacing lumber that is knotty, cross-grained, or that consists of various woods with different grains or hardness, and framed lumber, where the planing must be done with and across the grain. Usually this required special planers whose cutterheads were set at an angle to the feed, such as Bentel & Margedant Co.'s No. 44 Diagonal Surface Planer.

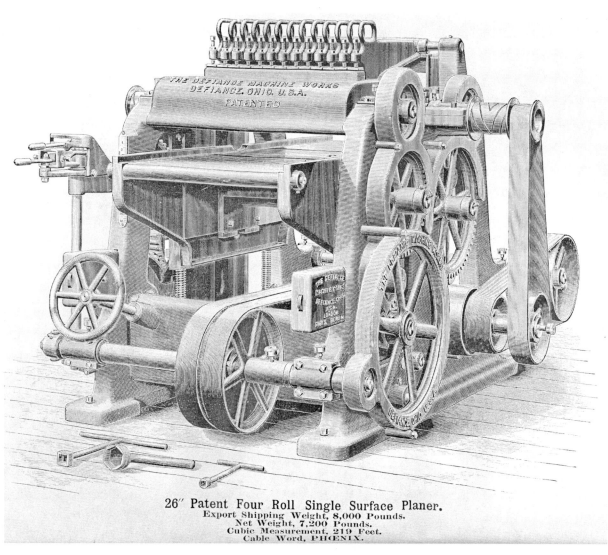

26″ Patent Four Roll Single Surface Planer.
Export Shipping Weight, 8,000 Pounds.
Net Weight, 7,200 Pounds.
Cubic Measurement, 219 Feet.
Cable Word, PHŒNIX.

Fig. 2-1: 26" Planer. Defiance Machine Works, Catalogue No. 200 1910.

YANKEE CYLINDER PLANING MACHINE.

EXTRA.

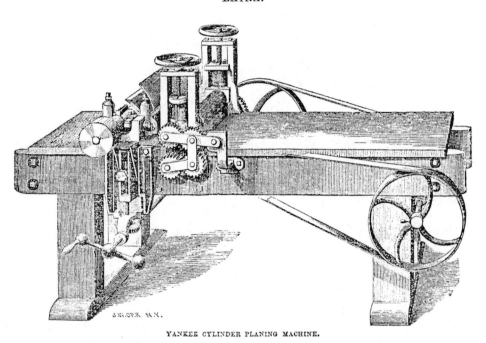

YANKEE CYLINDER PLANING MACHINE.

Fig. 2-2: Yankee Cylinder Planing Machine. J. A. Fay & Co., 1856 Catalog. The Upper Rolls Were Equipped With Goodyear's Patent Rubber Machine Springs. The Wood Framed Machine Was Double Belted.

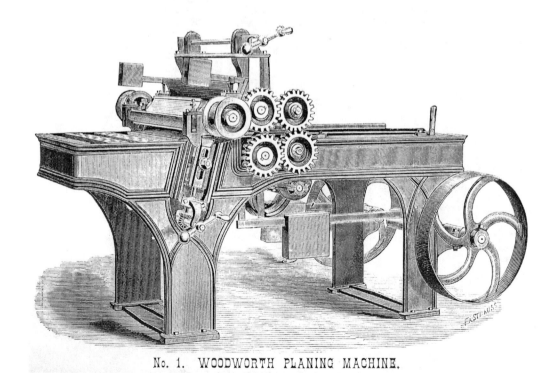

No. 1. WOODWORTH PLANING MACHINE.

Fig. 2-3: No. 1 Woodworth Planing Machine. Richardson, Meriam & Co., 1867 Catalog.

S. A. WOODS MACHINE CO'S

24

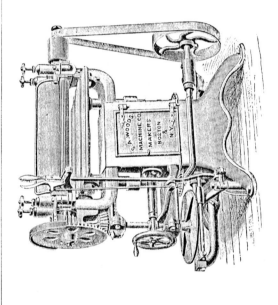

S. A. Woods Machine Co's Improved Panel Planer.

WITH FRICTION FEED.

For Planing Door-Panels, Furniture, Organ and Piano Work, and general Surfacing on thin or light stock, where especial nicety of work is desired.

TO WORK 20 INCHES WIDE AND 4 INCHES THICK, WEIGHT, 800 POUNDS.

WE take pleasure in introducing to notice our newly designed Panel Planer, which has many points of superiority over other machines of its class. The frame with the cylinder-boxes is cast in one piece with a hollow pedestal, the design being very neat in appearance, compact and solid. The cylinder with journals is made from a solid cast-steel forging, perfectly fitted and accurately balanced, and provided with our Patent Self-Oiling Boxes. The bed is raised or lowered for different thicknesses of stock by means of a hand-wheel conveniently placed at the side of the machine. A novel and

practical friction-feed is applied, being controlled by a lever, which by slight changes of position will produce a range of feed varying from 20 to 40 feet per minute, at the will of the operator, who is enabled to change from fast to slow or vice versa when a portion of the stock may be cross-grained, without the intervention of cones or belts, only one belt being required. A movement of the lever past the centre-stop, produces the reverse-feed for "backing out" the stock when desired. This machine is made with our customary care, and invariably put in practical operation before leaving the shop.

Fig. 2-4: Improved Panel Planer. S. A. Woods Machine Co., June 1, 1876 Catalog. Frame With Cutterhead Boxes Cast In One Piece With A Hollow Pedestal, Yoke, Cutterhead Of Solid Cast Steel Forging; Double Screw; Friction Variable Feed 20-40 fpm And Reverse Feed.

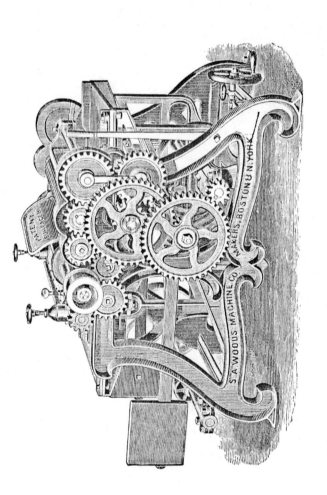

S. A. Woods Machine Co's Patent Improved Shop Surface Planer.

PLANES 24, 27 OR 30 INCHES WIDE AND 5 INCHES THICK. WEIGHT, 2000 TO 2200 POUNDS.

SEE DESCRIPTION OPPOSITE.

HE receiving pulleys on cylinder are $4\frac{1}{4}$ inches in diameter for 4-inch belt, and should make 3800 revolutions per minute. The belting required for this machine is as follows: to drive feed-works, $8\frac{8}{12}$ feet of 3-inch, and $9\frac{4}{12}$ feet of $2\frac{1}{2}$-inch.

A counter-shaft will be furnished to order when desired, at lowest market price. In ordering this, the speed and size of pulleys on main line must be given.

Fig. 2-5: Improved Shop Surface Planer. S.A.Woods Machine Co.,June 1, 1876 Catalog. Girded Construction With Wedge Bed.

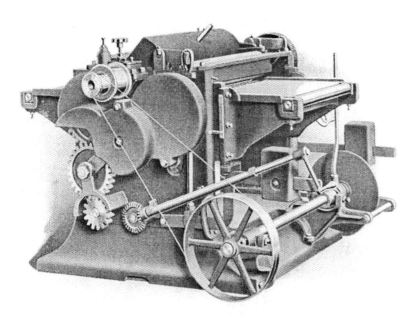

30 x 6 Crescent Variable Feed Surfacer
(Patent applied for)

Fig. 2-6: 30 x 6-inch Variable Feed Planer. Crescent Machine Co., 1912 Catalog.

30 x 6 Crescent Variable Feed Surfacer
(Patent applied for)

Fig. 2-6

Direct Motor Drive Single Surfacers

Direct Motor Drive Ball-Bearing Single Surfacers, built in 18 and 24″ with two rates of feeds.

Fig. 2-7: Direct Motor Drive Single Surfacer. Sidney Machine Tool Co., Circa 1924 Brochure.

"Every User
Is a Booster"

"Oliver" No. 361
Single Surface Planer
With One-Piece Inclined Bed
Supported by One-Piece Wedge

Dial Indicator for Thickness of Cut
Hand Lever Brake for Cylinder
One-Piece Cabinet Base
One-Piece Top Housing
One-Piece Bed and Wedge

Manufactured by

Oliver Machinery Co.
Grand Rapids, Mich., U. S. A.

BRANCH SALES OFFICES:
New York, St. Louis, Minneapolis, Los Angeles, San Francisco,
Chicago, Denver, Salt Lake City, Seattle, Detroit and Cleveland.

Fig. 2-8: No. 361 Single Surface Planer. Oliver Machinery Co., Circa 1949 Catalog.

25

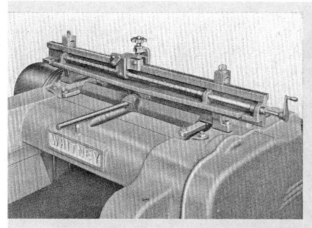

Showing hand feed screw on Grinder Bar for travel of electric grinder and jointing device along knife edge.

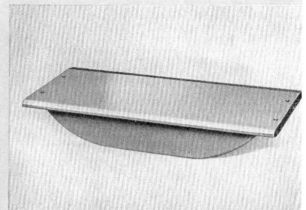

CENTER TABLE—Showing sturdy casting, depth of ribs and hardened and ground face.

CONTROLS

- Cutterhead and feed motor controls are conveniently located at left front of machine

- Magnetic switches and wiring panel, readily accessible, are completely enclosed in recess in rear of planer

- Selection of feeds is by Micro-feed Selector operated by handwheel directly below motor controls at front of planer

Section thru cutterhead showing knife setting adjustment and Whitney tapered knife clamps. Also position of chipbreaker and pressure bar.

CAPACITY

- Planes stock 1/16" to 8" in thickness, up to full 24" width. Single pieces as short as 13" or 3" when butted may be planed

- Rates of Feed: 20 to 60 feet per minute. Any feed desired between these limits

---

OTHER WOODWORKING MACHINES BY WHITNEY

Single and Double Planers—Automatic and Hand Shapers—Tilting Arbor Saw Bench—Horizontal Bit Mortiser—Scrapers—Back Knife Lathes

Fig. 2-9: No. 105 Single Surfacer With Removable, Hardened Center Table. Baxter D. Whitney & Son, Circa 1930s Brochure.

No. 0 IMPROVED PANEL PLANER.

Fig. 2-10: No. 0 Improved Panel Planer. L. Power & Co., Catalog, 1888.

Greenlee

NO. 110 SIX-ROLL SINGLE PLANER

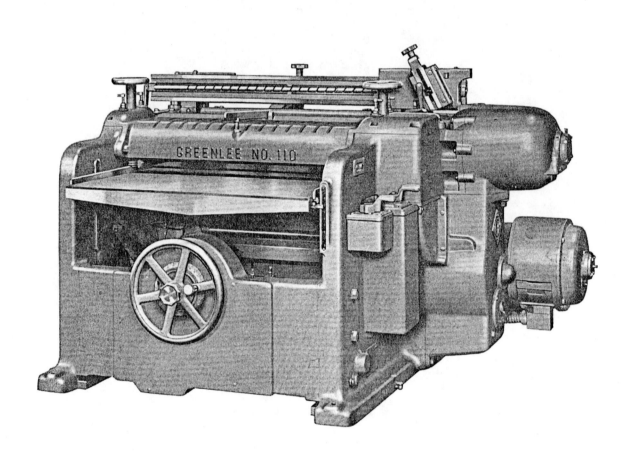

Fig. 2-11: No. 110 Six-Roll Single Planer. Greenlee Bros. & Co., Circa 1944 Catalog.

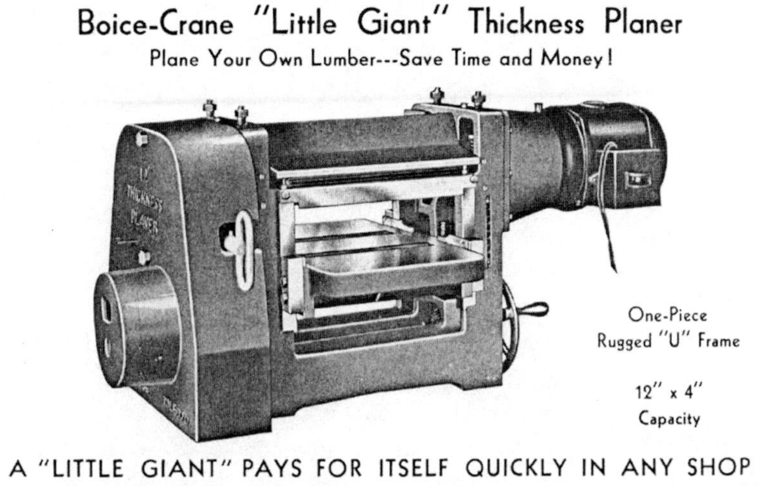

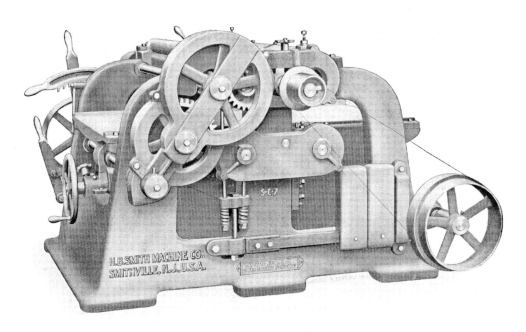

Fig. 2-12: "Little Giant" Bench Planer. Boice-Crane Co., Catalog M-1 1937. $198.

No. 30-A CABINET OR SMOOTHING SURFACER
Right-side Quartering View

Fig. 2-13: No. 30-A Cabinet Or Smoothing Surfacer. Patented July 2, 1901. H. B. Smith Machine Co., 1902 55th Ed. Catalog. Cutterhead Double Belted. A Limiting Bar Is Run Across The Machine To Prevent Too Heavy A Cut For The Cutterhead.

No. 10. SURFACE PLANER.

Fig. 2-14: No. 10 Surface Planer. C. B. Rogers & Co., May 1883 Catalog.

SMALL CYLINDER PLANING MACHINE.

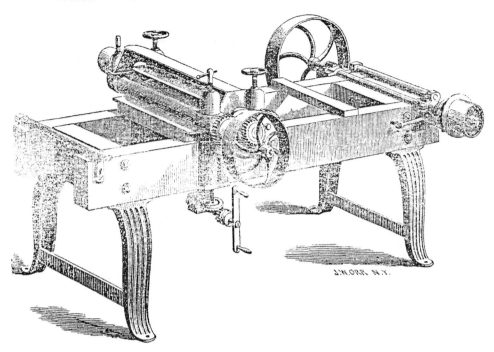

Fig. 2-15: Small Cylinder Planing Machine. J. A. Fay & Co., 1856 Catalog. Available As 20, 22, & 24 x 4". Wood Frame, Iron Legs, Two Pressure Feed Rolls, And A 5" Cutterhead. It has a convenient arrangement for adjusting the cutterhead to the thickness of the work, and an apparatus for stopping and starting feed. The Cutterhead Unit And Feed Rolls Were Raised. Spring Tension On Top Feed Rolls.

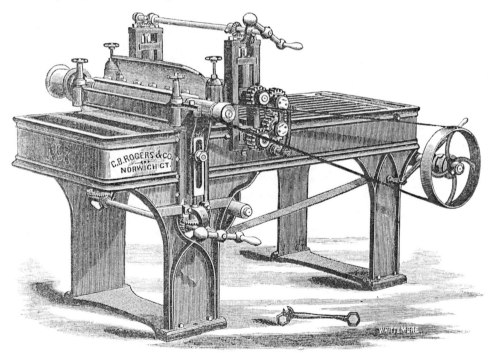

No. 7. CYLINDER PLANER, IRON FRAME.

Fig. 2-16: No. 7 Planer. C. B. Rogers & Co., May 1883 Catalog.

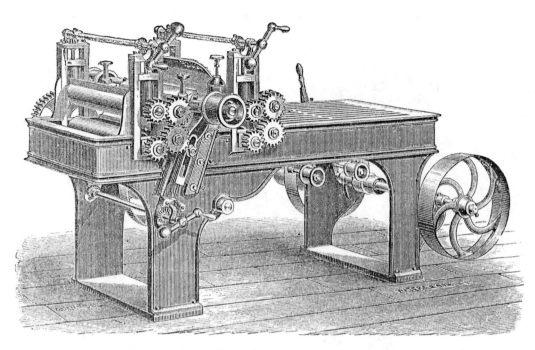

No. 8. SURFACE PLANER, FOUR ROLL.

Fig. 2-17: No. 8 Surfacer Planer. C. B. Rogers & Co., May 1883 Catalog.

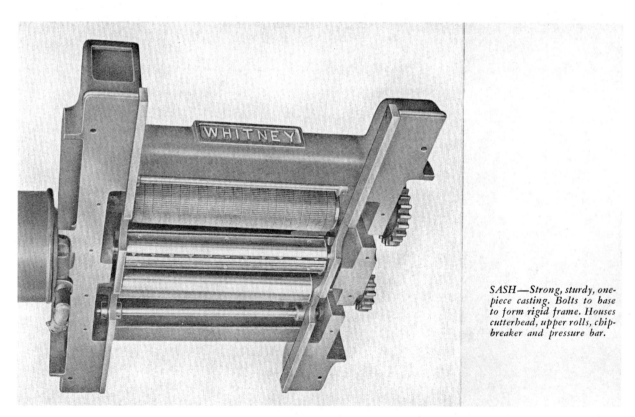

SASH—Strong, sturdy, one-piece casting. Bolts to base to form rigid frame. Houses cutterhead, upper rolls, chipbreaker and pressure bar.

Fig. 2-18: No. 105 Sash With Feed Rolls, Cutterhead, Chipbreaker & Pressure Bar. Baxter D. Whitney & Son, Circa 1930s Brochure.

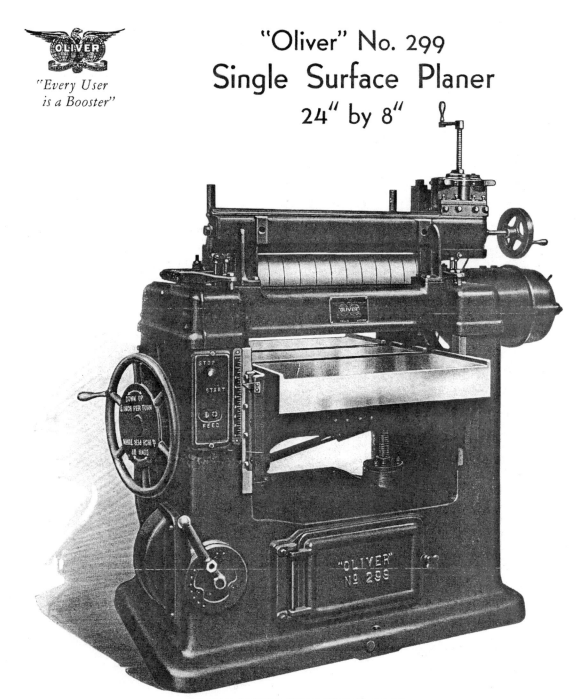

"Oliver" No. 299
Single Surface Planer
24" by 8"

"Every User is a Booster"

NO. 299-D "OLIVER" SINGLE SURFACE PLANER
Front View of complete machine with Sectional Chipbreaker, Sectional Roll and Permanently Located Knife Grinding and Jointing Attachment. Note that all controls, both electrical and mechanical, are conveniently concentrated directly in front of the operator.

SECTIONAL UPPER IN-FEED ROLL
Note the positive Drive and the Fool-Proof Construction.

Manufactured by

Oliver Machinery Company
Grand Rapids, Mich., U.S.A.

BRANCH SALES OFFICES:
New York, Cleveland, Detroit, Indianapolis, Chicago, St. Louis, Minneapolis, Denver, Salt Lake City, Seattle, Portland, San Francisco, Los Angeles.

Fig. 2-19: No. 299 Single Surfacer. 24 x 8, Variable Speed 15 to 60 fpm By Turn Of A Dial. Oliver Machinery Co., Feb. 1948 Brochure.

24=INCH MONITOR SURFACE PLANER No. 41
With Patent Triangular Shear=Knife Cutterhead

Fig. 2-20: No. 41 Monitor Surface Planer. Triangular Shear Knife Cutterhead Rises And Lowers. One Piece Cast-Iron Frame. Bentel & Margedant Co., Catalogue K, Circa 1890.

F. H. CLEMENT CO.'S
No. 4, Heavy Double Belted Furniture Planer.

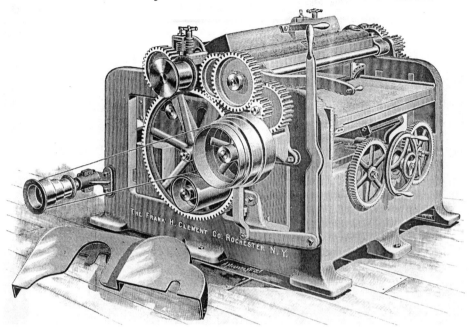

Fig. 2-21: No. 4 Heavy Double Belted Furniture Planer. Wedge Bed. Frank H. Clement Co. American Wood Working Machine. Co., First Edition Catalog, 1898.

ROWLEY & HERMANCE CO.'S
"Prize" Pony or Panel Planer.

Fig. 2-22: Prize Pony Or Panel Planer. Patented May 9, 1871 & Sept. 23, 1879. Available As 18 & 24 x 6. 1/16 Minimum Thickness. One Piece Cast-Iron Frame. Rowley & Hermance Co., 9th Ed. Catalog 1897.

Countershaft.

Fig. 2-23: "Jewel" Planer. Available As 16 x 6 & 20 x 6. 1/4" Minimum Thickness. American Saw Mill Machinery Co., Catalog B 1914.

ROWLEY & HERMANCE CO.'S
"Peacemaker" Double Belted Single Surfacer.

Fig. 2-24: Peacemaker Double Belted Single Surfacer. The Model Had A New Device For Quickly And Securely Clamping The Table To The Frame. The Upper Infeed Roll Was Fluted And Weighted And Connected By Improved Compensating Weight Levers So Equal Pressure Was Applied The Entire Width Of The Machine. Rowley & Hermance Co., 9th Ed. Catalog 1897.

Fig. 2-25: First Whitney Planer, 1846. Baxter D. Whitney & Son, Circa 1905 Catalog.

Fig. 2-26: Silver Medal Planer. Baxter D. Whitney Co. 1866.

BASE — Integral Construction
Sturdy, one-piece, rectangular casting for rigidity and the maintenance of accuracy.

UPPER and LOWER WEDGES
Cross members cast integrally with wedges for rigidity and permanency of alignment.

Fig. 2-27: Planer Frame Showing Wedges. Baxter D. Whitney & Son Co. No. 29A & 32A Single Surface Planers Brochure, Circa 1930s.

**FRAME AND WEDGES OF THE WHITNEY
SINGLE PLANER**
Showing the simplicity and sturdy construction of the Whitney.

Fig. 2-28: Planer Frame & Wedge Design. Baxter D. Whitney & Son Co. No. 29 & 32 Single Surface Planers Brochure, Circa 1935.

WHITNEY No. 32A SINGLE SURFACE PLANER *with belted feed driven
from cutterhead motor.*
*See front of bulletin for No. 32A Planer with Variable Speed Feed Unit
direct-connected to feed shaft.*

Fig. 2-29: No. 32A Single Surface Planer. Variable Speed 20-80 fpm. Baxter D. Whitney & Son Co. 1930s Brochure.

No. 9. SURFACE PLANER.

Fig. 2-30: No. 9 Surface Planer. C. B. Rogers & Co., May 1883 Catalog.

S. A. Woods Machine Co's Patent Improved Endless Bed Planer,

WITH PATENT COMBINATION PRESSURE, CHIP-BREAKER AND SHAVING-GUARD.

PLANES 24, 27 OR 30 INCHES WIDE AND 10 INCHES THICK.   WEIGHT, 2700 TO 3000 POUNDS.

SEE DESCRIPTION OPPOSITE.

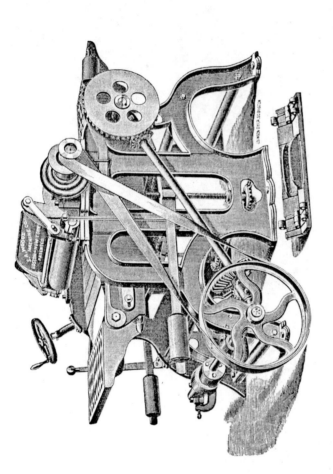

A COUNTER-SHAFT will be furnished to order when desired, at lowest market price. In ordering this, the speed and size of pulleys on main line must be given.

The receiving pulleys on cylinder are $4\frac{1}{4}$ inches in diameter for 4-inch belt, and should make 4000 revolutions per minute. The belting required for this machine is as follows: for feed-works, $9\frac{8}{12}$ feet of $2\frac{1}{4}$-inch.

Fig. 2-31: Improved Endless Bed Surfacer. Patented June 2, 1874. S.A. Woods Machine Co., June 1, 1876 Catalog.

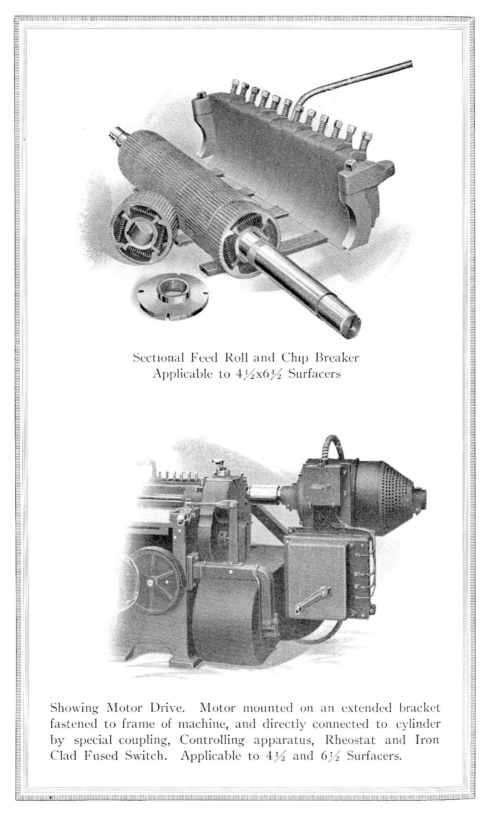

Sectional Feed Roll and Chip Breaker
Applicable to 4½x6½ Surfacers

Showing Motor Drive. Motor mounted on an extended bracket
fastened to frame of machine, and directly connected to cylinder
by special coupling, Controlling apparatus, Rheostat and Iron
Clad Fused Switch. Applicable to 4½ and 6½ Surfacers.

Fig. 2-32: No. 4 1/2 Single Surfacer. American Wood Working Machine Co. 10th Ed.
Catalog, 1915. 24 x 7.1/16" Minimum Thickness. Feed Driven Direct From Cutterhead.
Two speeds 18 and 32 fpm. Binder Pulley And Lever Starts And Stops Feed.

F. H. CLEMENT CO.'S
No. 2½ Double Belted Surfacer, Improved.

Fig. 2-33: No. 2 1/2 Improved Double Belted Surfacer. Frank H. Clement Co., American Wood Working Machine Co., First Edition Catalog, 1898.

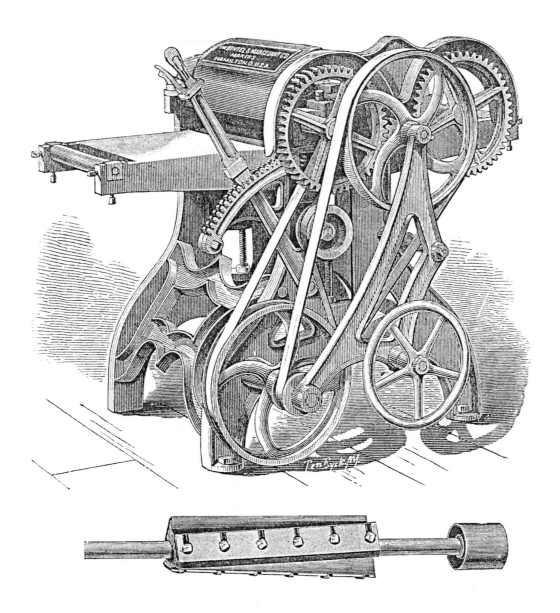

24=INCH HAMILTON SURFACE PLANER No. 42

With Patent Triangular Shear=knife Cutterhead.

Fig. 2-34: No. 42 Hamilton Surface Planer. 24 x 6. Shear Knife Cutterhead. Feed Rolls Driven Directly From Cutterhead. Heavy Open Frame Bolted Together. Long, One Piece, Cast-Iron Bed Slides On Gibbed Ways In Frame. Rises And Lowers By Two Heavy Screws. Six Feed Rolls. Bentel & Margedant Co., Catalogue K, Circa 1890.

No. 25-A SURFACE PLANING MACHINE SINGLE
(Outfeeding End view showing Divided Chip-Breaker and Belt-Binder)

Fig. 2-35: No. 25-A Single Surfacer. Patented July 2, 1901. Power Transmitted From The Infeed To The Outfeed Rolls By All Steel Roller Link Chain. H. B. Smith Machine Co., 1902 55th Ed. Catalog.

26 AND 30-INCH HEAVY SMOOTHING AND FINISHING PLANER No. 45

Fig. 2-36: No. 45 Heavy Smoothing And Finishing Planer. Available As 26, 30, & 36 x 6. Wedge Bed. Double Cored Frame. Wide Base. One Piece Forged Steel Cutterhead And Shaft. Triangular Shear Knife Head. Gear Covers Removed And On Ground. Bentel & Margedant Co., Catalogue K, Circa 1890.

The SIDNEY MACHINE TOOL COMPANY

EACH MACHINE TESTED at the cylinder speed of 4500 R. P. M. must plane stock down to ⅛ inch thick without tearing or clipping ends.

Designed for heavy shop work as well as finest cabinet shop, furniture factory, or other grades of high class planing of wood of all styles.

All Famous planers fitted with semi-high speed cylinder knives. Three or four knife heads furnished at slight extra cost if desired.

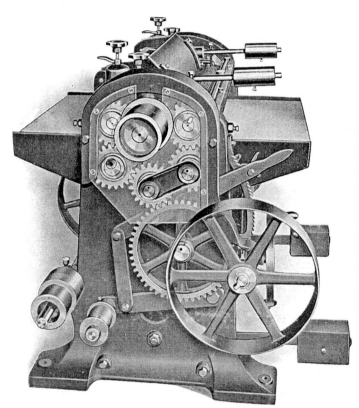

Fig. 366 and 370 Double Belted, Four Roll Driven Type

SPECIFICATIONS

	362	368	366	370
Figure number	362	368	366	370
Will plane stock up to	18 x 8 inches	24 x 8 inches	24 x 8 inches	26 x 8 inches
Cylinder journals	2 x 6½ inches	2 x 6½ inches	2 x 8½ inches	2 x 8½ inches
Width of cylinder belts	5 inches	5 inches	5 inches	5 inches
Width of feed belt	2 inches	2 inches	2 inches	2 inches
Tight and loose pulley sizes	10 x 5 inches	10 x 5½ inches	10 x 9 inches	10 x 9 inches
Speed of countershaft	900 R. P. M.	900 R. P. M.	900 R. P. M.	900 R. P. M.
Speed of cylinder head	4200 R. P. M.	4200 R. P. M.	4200 R. P. M.	4200 R. P. M.
Floor space, countershaft not included	33 x 48 inches	36 x 52 inches	40 x 60 inches	42 x 64 inches
Horse power recommended	3 H. P.	5 H. P.	5 to 7½ H. P.	7½ to 10 H. P.
Weight, crated for shipment	1425 lbs.	1525 lbs.	2550 lbs.	2750 lbs.
Weight, boxed for export shipment	1950 lbs.	2100 lbs.	3150 lbs.	3350 lbs.
Telegraph code name	Fir	Firland	Pyan	Pyanl

EQUIPMENT

Each machine is furnished with complete countershaft, one pair of knives with bolts, and the necessary wrenches.

Fig. 2-37: Single & Double Belted Surfacers, Sidney Machine Tool Co., Circa 1924 Brochure.

Improved Heavy Surfacing Machine.

Fig. 2-38: Improved Heavy Surfacing Machine. Available As 16, 20, 24, & 28 x 4. 1/4" Minimum Thickness. Open Frame Bolted Together. Forged, Solid Steel, Cutterhead. Two Sides Tapped. Cast Steel Links And Gears. H. B. Smith Machine Co., 1887. Catalog.

Variable Feed

Fig. 774. American No. 4½ Single Furniture Planer

Fig. 2-39: American No. 4 1/2 Single Furniture Planer. Wedge Bed. American Wood Working Machinery Co. Ninth Ed. Catalog, Circa 1909.

Figure 7651   *Figure 7641*

Fig. 2-40: American No. 1 Single Surfacer. Available As 16, 20 & 24 x 6. 1/16" Minimum Thickness. American Wood Working Machinery Co., 10th Ed. Catalog 1915.

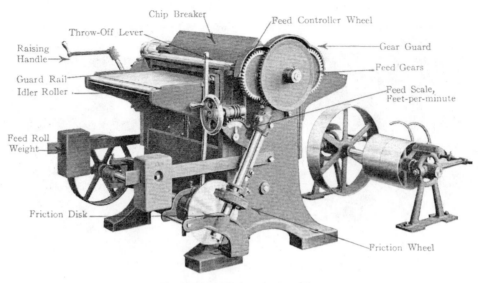

Variable Feed Planers Nos. 218 and 224
(Patented)

Fig. 2-41: Nos. 218 & 224 Planers. Crescent Machine Co., 1921 Catalog.

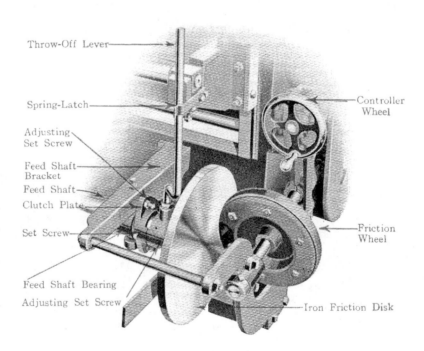

Variable Friction Feed for Planers

Fig. 2-42: Variable Feed Mechanism. Crescent Machine Co., 1921 Catalog.

Crescent Knife Jointing Attachment

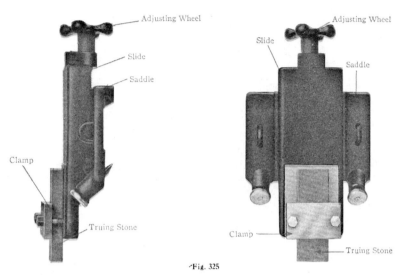

Fig. 325

Knife Jointing Attachment. (Fig. 325) A small attachment for jointing the knives is also very desirable and can be used in the same slide as the grinder. The use of the jointing attachment eliminates much trouble incident to setting knives and when it is used the operator may be sure each knife will do its full share of the cutting.

Code Word for Jointing Attachment complete with bridge, but without motor driven grinder, Matub.

Code Word for Knife Jointing Attachment, when furnished in connection with motor driven knife grinder, Medon.

Motor Driven Planer
Motor Attached Direct to Planer Head

Fig. 238

THIS style of drive requires a motor running at high speed and makes a very desirable outfit. (Fig. 238). Because of difficulty in driving the feed we do not recommend this style of drive on the No. 118 and No. 124 planers, but the other planers in the Crescent line are well adapted to it. There is no extra charge for motor base or flexible coupling on the No. 218, No. 224 and 26″ planers. but on the No. 324 and No. 424 planers and matchers a slight additional charge is made for motor bracket and flexible coupling.

Fig. 2-43: Motor Driven Planers. Crescent Machine Co., Aug. 25, 1924 Brochure.

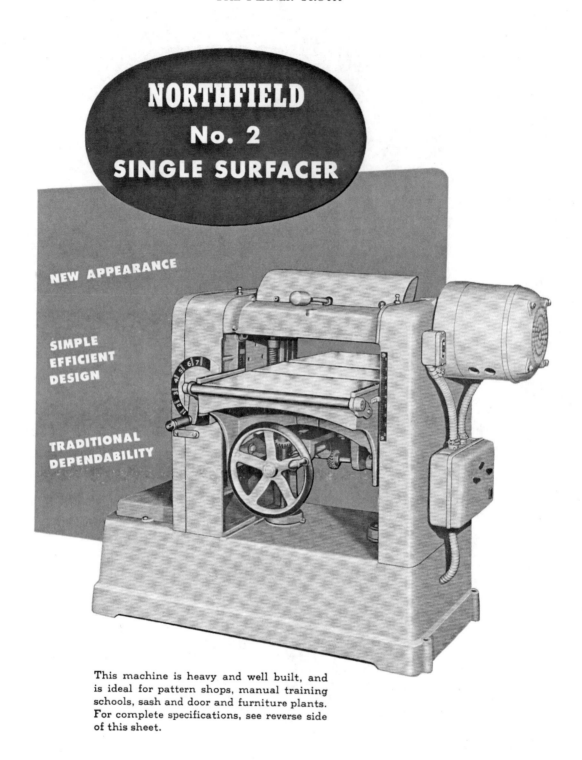

NORTHFIELD
No. 2
SINGLE SURFACER

NEW APPEARANCE

SIMPLE
EFFICIENT
DESIGN

TRADITIONAL
DEPENDABILITY

This machine is heavy and well built, and
is ideal for pattern shops, manual training
schools, sash and door and furniture plants.
For complete specifications, see reverse side
of this sheet.

Northfield FOUNDRY & MACHINE CO.
★ ★ ★ NORTHFIELD, MINNESOTA, U.S.A.

Fig. 2-44: No. 2 Single Surfacer. 18 x 8. 1/8" Minimum. 1/4" Maximum Cut. Feed From Separate 1/3 hp Motor
Variable Speed 26 To 60 fpm. Power Transmitted To Top Two Feed Rolls By Sprockets And Chain. Northfield
Foundry & Machine Co., Jan. 1957 Sectional Catalog.

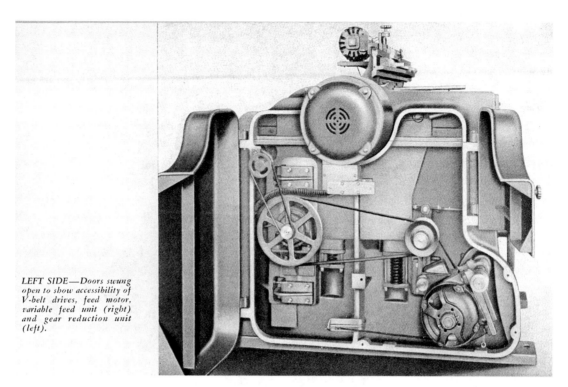

LEFT SIDE—Doors swung open to show accessibility of V-belt drives, feed motor, variable feed unit (right) and gear reduction unit (left).

Fig. 2-45: No. 105. Left Side Showing V-Belt Drive, Feed Motor, Variable Feed Unit, And Gear Reduction Unit. Baxter D. Whitney & Son Co. Circa 1930s Brochure.

NO. 2 HEAVY PANEL PLANER.
To Plane 24 and 32 inches wide and 6 inches thick.

Fig. 2-46: No. 2 Heavy Panel Planer. Double Belted. L. Power & Co., Catalog, 1888.

No. 61
"Oliver" Single Cylinder Surfacer
Continued

"OLIVER" No. 61 FOUR ROLL, SINGLE CYLINDER, DOUBLE BELTED
CABINET SURFACER
View from Left Hand Side.

Fig. 2-47: No. 61 Four Roll Cabinet Planer. Double Belted. Oliver Machinery Co., Catalog No. 21, Circa 1920.

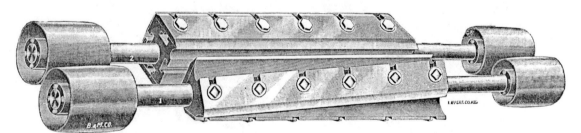

Patent Triangular Shearknife and Four-Slotted Cutterheads

Fig. 2-48: Triangular And Square cutterheads. All Sides Slotted & Lipped. Bentel & Margedant Co., Catalogue K, Circa 1890.

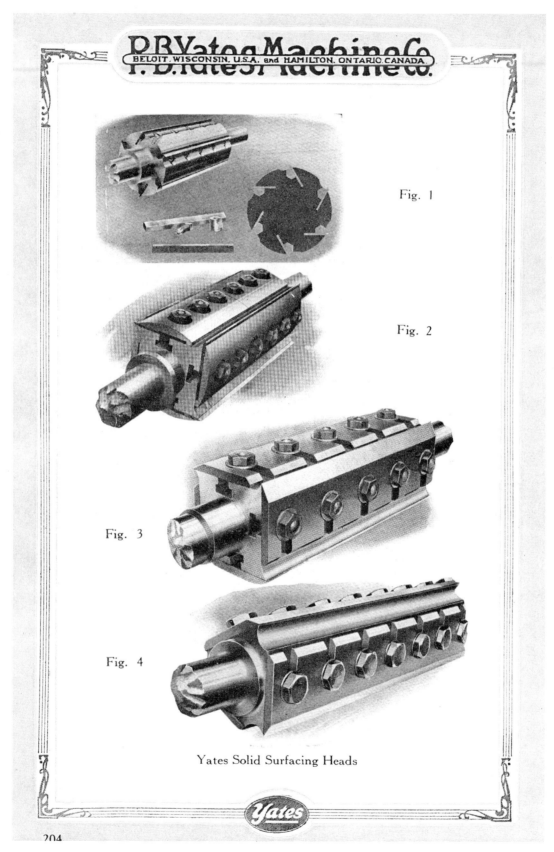

Yates Solid Surfacing Heads

Fig. 2-49: Cutterheads. P. B. Yates Machine Co., Catalog No. 14, Circa 1917.

53

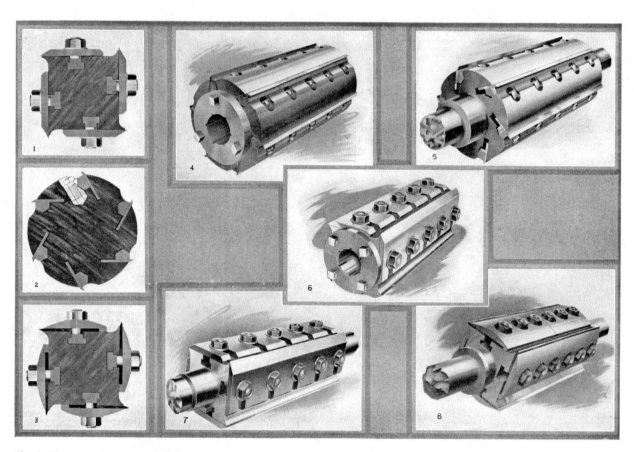

Fig. 2-50: Cutterheads. Solid Steel Forgings. P. B. Yates Machine Co., Dec. 1, 1917 Brochure.

"Oliver" Circular Safety Cylinder
Continued

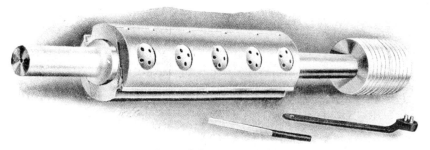

(Patented January 21, 1908).
Halftone showing a complete Cylinder with Wrench and Knife Setting Tool.
May be supplied with two or four knives.

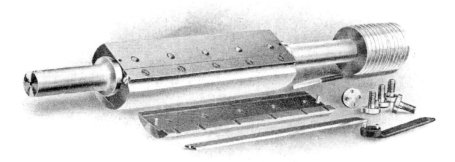

Halftone Showing Cylinder Dismantled.
Can be furnished with divided caps for using moulding knives.
The "Oliver" is the Original Safety Cylinder. Don't Select Substitutes!
Complete description on request.

"Oliver" Double Belted Circular Safety Cylinder for Surface Planers.

Fig. 2-51: Two Knife Round Cutterhead. Slab Knife Holder Type. Oliver Machinery Co., Catalog No. 21, Circa 1920.

WHITNEY 4-KNIFE ROUND CUTTERHEAD
Showing method of clamping and adjusting the knives, and the Sectional Chipbreaker in action.

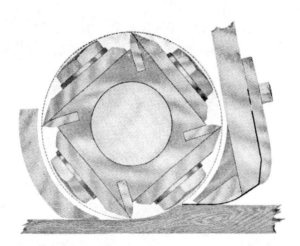

WHITNEY 4-KNIFE SQUARE CUTTERHEAD
Showing the hardened steel lips inserted in the cutterhead, and the Flexible Spring Chipbreaker in action.

Fig. 2-52: Square & Round Cutterheads. Tool Steel Forgings. With Knife Set-Up & Sectional & Spring Chipbreakers. Baxter D. Whitney & Son Co. No. 29 & 32 Single Surface Planers Brochure, Circa 1935.

View from Gear-Case Side of No. 110 Planer with Four-Speed Feed Motor. Gear Case is dust tight and Feed Gears run in oil.

head out of balance due to any slight difference in position. Screws for adjusting the knives to the cutting circle are so designed that they will not bind, and they fit the holes so closely that dust can not work down and clog their movement. There are no tapped holes in the head to cause trouble from stripped threads, which would have to be repaired in such a manner as to destroy the balance. Gib screws are threaded into the knife gibs, and the adjusting screws into sleeves, so that either can be readily replaced when necessary to do so.

Chip-breakers Both sectional and flexible chipbreakers are available for this machine. Each type has a heavy cast bar mounted on rings which completely encircle the trunnions on the head bearing housings. This construction insures great rigidity and a concentric action relative to the cutting cylinder, permitting close operation to the knives with no danger of injuring them. Unlike most chipbreakers of the concentric or the link type, this one will not bind on the stock. A carefully worked out lift, which is simplicity itself, cor-

rectly sets the bar at the proper height for the amount of cut being taken, but only high enough for the stock to enter easily without sacrificing the required pressure. Thus, the ideal chipbreaker is realized, safely working close to the cutting circle, requiring a minimum of space, and keeping the material firmly on the platen while allowing it to feed through without interruption or atttention and without any effort on the part of the operator.

Dust proof, lubricated construction, combined with the lift described above, form a sectional chipbreaker which works equally well on strip or panel stock. The easy-acting, hardened steel fingers have one-quarter inch independent yield and adjust themselves to suit the material. They project over the lower edge of the bar on the side toward the head so that dust and chips cannot enter. A felt wick distributes oil as it is needed, but not enough to get on the stock. Fingers and springs are readily accessible without removing the bar from the machine. Edges of the fingers are rounded to prevent damage to stock.

On the flexible chipbreaker the spring is slotted to equalize the pressure at all points and is reversible so that it may be used until both edges are worn out. The method of holding it is so designed that the bending does not take place along a line through the middle only. The entire spring is flexible across the width from edge to edge, and this greatly increases the useful life of the spring.

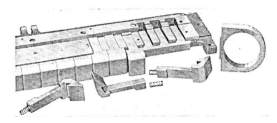

Heavy one-piece Chipbreaker Bar with steel retaining plates for fingers and springs. The hardened steel fingers are designed so that they project up over the lower edge of the bar to prevent chips and dust from wedging in between the fingers and the bar.

[4]

Fig. 2-53: No. 110 Six-Roll Single Planer. Wedge Bed. Sectional Chipbreaker. Greenlee Bros. & Co., Circa 1944 Catalog.

57

"OLIVER" PLANER KNIVES FOR SURFACE PLANERS

We supply these for either Circular or Square Cylinders as required. For the Circular Cylinders we furnish the special air hardening steel knives referred to above. For the Square Cylinder we carry a large variety of laid knives of excellent quality. All knives are guaranteed.

Fig. 2-54: Slotted Knife For Square Cutterhead Surface Planers. Oliver Machinery Co., Catalog No. 21, Circa 1920.

Fig. 7421. American No. 112 Single and Double Surfacers

Fig. 2-55: No. 112 Single Surfacer. Double Belted. Cutterhead Solid Steel Forging, Lipped On Two Sides, Slotted On All Four Sides, Two Knives. American Wood Working Machine Co. Ninth Ed. Catalog Circa 1909.

Norris Patent Improved Diagonal Planer and Polishing Machine.

Capacity, 500 to 600 Doors in Ten Hours.

Fig. 2-56: Norris Patent Improved Diagonal Planer With Optional Polishing Head. Rowley & Hermance Co., 9th Ed. Catalog 1897.

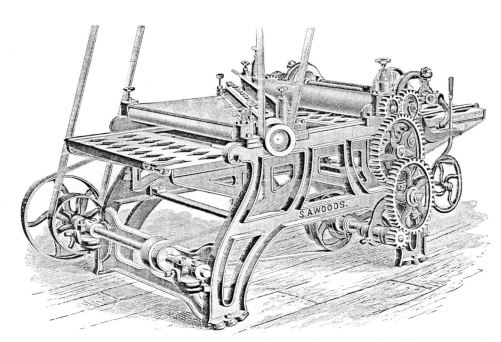

S. A. Woods Machine Co's Improved Door Planer, with Diagonal Cylinder.

Fig. 2-57: Improved Door Planer. Diagonal Cutterhead. S.A.Woods Machine Co., June 1, 1876 Catalog.

20=INCH DIAGONAL SURFACE PLANER No. 44

With Patent Triangular Shear=knife Cutterhead.

Fig. 2-58: No. 44 Diagonal Surface Planer With Shear Knife Cutterhead. Similar To No. 42 But The Cutterhead And The Pressure Bars Positions Differ. Bentel & Margedant Co., Catalogue K, Circa 1890.

TELEGRAPHIC CIPHER
To Plane 16 Inches Wide, ...
To Plane 20 Inches Wide, ...
To Plane 24 Inches Wide, ...

No. 2 Surface Planing Machine.

Fig. 2-59: No. 2 Surface Planing Machine. Available As 16, 20 & 24 x 6. Forged Crucible Steel Cutterhead With Lips To Break Chips. J. A. Fay & Egan Co., Catalogue Series L Circa 1901.

NO. 151 SINGLE SURFACER—FOUR ROLLS.

Fig. 2-60: No. 151 Single Surfacer. "Sometimes Called A Pony Planer Because It Is The Smallest Surfacer We Build." Berlin Machine Works, Catalog No. 15, 1908.

GIANT TRIPLE 60-INCH COMBINED HAND AND POWER FEED PLANER No. 52

Fig. 2-61: No. 52 Power Feed Planer, 60-inch. Also Built As A Combined Planer, Jointer, & Molder. Largest & Widest Hand & Power Surface Planer Ever Built. Heavy Forged Steel Cutterhead Measures 8 ft. 6 in. Long. Bentel & Margedant Co., Catalogue K, Circa 1890.

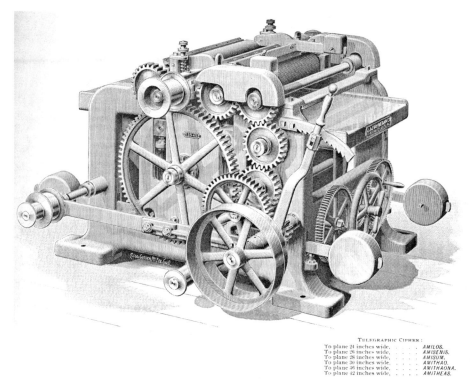

Improved No. 4 Heavy Planer and Smoother.

Fig. 2-62: Improved No. 4 Heavy Planer And Smoother. Available As 24, 26, 28, 30, 36, & 42 x 6. J.A. Fay & Egan Co., Catalogue Series L Circa 1901.

Fig. 2-63: No. 19 Improved Extra Heavy Planer And Smoother. Available As 24, 26, 30, 36, & 42 x 6. Steel Spring Shoe For Chipbreaker. Patented Dec. 19, 1899, Feb. 6, 1900, & May 8, 1900, J.A. Fay & Egan Co., Catalogue Series L Circa 1901.

Chapter 3

SAFETY

READ THIS FIRST

The modern roll-feed single surface planer is one of the safest woodworking machines to operate because the knives, gears, and other moving parts are enclosed, and the lumber is power-fed. But they are still dangerous. All planers, vintage or new, should be respected and the following rules must always be observed.

SAFETY

1. Wear an approved safety shield, goggles, or glasses. Common eyeglasses are only impact-resistant.
2. Before operating the planer, remove all rings, watches, and other jewelry. Roll up sleeves above the elbows and tuck in shirts. Remove all loose clothing and confine long hair. Do not wear gloves.
3. Keep *all* guards in place. If missing or broken, have new ones fabricated or have repairs made.
4. Keep the area around the planer clean and free of scrap material, sawdust, oil, and other liquids to minimize the danger of tripping or slipping. Be sure all the tables and the planer itself are free of scraps, foreign material, and tools before operating. Make sure the area is well illuminated and provide adequate work space around the planer.
5. Avoid accidental starting.
6. Stand to the left or right side of the planer, out of line with the table while feeding lumber, a kickback can cause severe or even fatal injury. Make sure no one else is standing in line with the table.
7. When the feed roll takes hold of a board, let go of it. Always keep your hands at a safe distance from the feed rolls.
8. On short boards, never place your fingers on the edge or underside of the board. The sudden, downward force of the infeed roll can pinch them between the table and board.
9. Make sure to feed the board into the planer straight. If a board runs through a planer diagonally it may climb the edges of the table and jam the machine. If a long board should be started inadvertently in a diagonal direction, a quick sidewise pull or push at the start will straighten it.
10. If the board is short and wide, and begins to feed diagonally, stop the feed mechanism immediately and then the cutterhead. Wait until the cutterhead stops, and lower the bed until the board is freed. Remove the board, reset the table to its former height, and then start the cutterhead. Hold the lumber firmly with both hands, and start it straight through the planer.
11. When feeding several pieces side by side with a sectional roll, send them in straight and make sure they aren't touching.
12. If there is a shavings hood, be sure that the hood is in place and the fan started before you begin planing.
13. On vintage planers check that the feed pressure weights are properly set before planing.
14. Pay attention to what you are doing and don't horseplay around the planer.
15. Disconnect the planer from its power source before performing any service or maintenance work such as changing knives.

16. Keep knives sharp and clean.

17. Do not feed stacked boards through the planer, kickback can occur.

18. If lumber stops feeding, disengage or turn off the feed and turn off the power. Wait until the cutterhead has come to a dead stop before taking steps to free the lumber. Never adjust the cutting depth with the power on and lumber still in the planer; kickback can occur. Some planers have a reverse switch to turn the rollers backwards if lumber gets stuck in the machine.

19. Keep hands outside the planer. Never reach under the guards while the planer is running. Do not clean chips or sawdust away with hands, use a brush. The knives are sharp. Do not have any part of the hands under that part of the lumber that is over the table while starting a cut; the infeed roll will engage the board and can snap it down against the table causing a pinching action.

20. Do not plane boards with loose knots or with nails or any foreign material on its surface. Remember that nails, screws, etc., can be hidden beneath the surface of used lumber. Impact on these objects not only nicks and dulls the knives but can cause the knives to be pulled out and cause them to shatter against the chipbreaker or pressure bar.

21. Twisted or warped lumber should first be jointed smooth or semi-smooth on one surface so it will lie flat on the table before trying to plane a parallel surface. Not only will it yield a better finish but it's safer. Feed rolls will temporarily flatten a warped board. Serious lumber flaws cannot be removed by use of a planer alone.

22. Do not attempt to feed two boards side by side of unequal thickness on any planer not equipped with a sectional infeed feed roll and chipbreaker. The roll will only contact the highest board and kickback is possible.

23. Make all planer adjustments with the power off.

24. Do not leave a running planer unattended. Do not leave the planer until the cutterhead has come to a complete stop.

25. Never attempt to clean the planer while running. Disconnect the planer from the power source before cleaning.

26. Wood planers are designed for planing wood. Do not attempt to plane other materials.

27. Provide proper support for long boards both in the front and the rear.

Chapter 4

PLANER SYSTEM

The principal parts of a planer are: the supporting frame, the bed or table, the bed or idler rolls (sometimes called anti-friction rolls), the cutterhead, the feed rolls, the chipbreaker, the pressure bar, and the feed control mechanism.

The usual feeding system of a single surface planer consists of one powered infeed roll, a chipbreaker, the cutterhead, a pressure bar, one powered outfeed roll, and the idler bed rolls mounted directly beneath the feed rolls (Fig. 4-1). The upper rollers, chipbreaker, and pressure bar hold the wood down by a combination of their own weight and/or spring pressure or weights.

The rolls on the more sophisticated production planers are all powered to maintain uniformity of feed, reduce breakage, and avoid stoppages that cause burns from cutterheads and slipping rolls. Effectiveness of the feed is also improved if the rolls are of large diameter, corrugated, and mounted in multiples—two pairs of infeeding rolls are more effective than one pair. Some larger types have six powered feed rolls (Fig. 4-2), two pairs of infeed rolls and one pair of outfeed rolls or eight feed rolls (Fig. 4-3), two pair of each.

Commonly, the top infeed is corrugated and the bottom infeed roll solid and smooth. However, if the lumber is very uneven in thickness, or if it is fed in multiples across the width of the machine, the top roll may be of the sectional type (Fig. 4-4). These rolls have independent narrow sections spring-supported on an internal arbor so each section can yield as much as 3/4-inch independently.

To guarantee positive feed on very rough or wet lumber, some planers also have the bottom infeed roll corrugated and set a fraction of an inch above the bed. Machines handling dry, smooth, flat lumber have a smooth infeed roll barely raised above the bed.

The feed rolls are very heavy and strongly made. Typically their bearings, whether Babbitt, ball, or roller, are enclosed in cast-iron boxes or steel cases, which fit snugly into tracks or ways in the frame to keep them from twisting and are adjustable up or down (Fig. 4-5).

All the feed rolls are connected to each other and driven by gears (Fig. 4-6), belts (Fig. 4-7), or a chain link belt (Fig. 4-8) that engages with a gear, sprocket, or pulley on the shaft on which the motor is mounted or to which the drive belt is connected. On small machines, the feed mechanism is usually driven off the cutterhead (Fig. 4-9), but on large machines, it is driven by a separate motor (Fig. 4-10).

In either case, the feed rolls can be started and stopped independently of the cutterhead usually by a hand lever of some sort. Yates-American Machine Co.'s 1930 B-4 Direct Motor Driven Single Surfacer had a foot treadle which started and stopped the feed.

S. A. Woods Machine Co.'s 1876 Improved Panel Planer (Fig. 2-5) had a reverse feed and a variable feed operated from a friction disk. Crescent Machine Co.'s 1946 P-24 Planer featured a reverse feed. On modern machines, all gears and belts are enclosed or guarded. The rate of feed may be adjusted from 30 to 130 fpm.

INFEED ROLL

The function of the infeed roll, usually deeply corrugated in a helix lengthwise to assure a firm grip on the material, is to grab the board and pull it into the planer. The solid infeed roll can only handle one board thickness at a time (Fig. 4-11).

The backward force from the cutterhead is tremendous, so the infeed roll also has the task of keeping the board from flying back toward the operator. Though the infeed roll is set about 1/16" lower than the cutting circle, the marks left on the wood get planed off by the knives.

The infeed and the bed roll below revolve in opposite directions, and move the board forward at a uniform rate of speed, which can be regulated.

There are two ways of increasing the capacity of a planer: one is to increase the lineal speed of feed, the other is to provide a way of feeding several pieces of varying thickness through the machine at the same time. The first has the serious objection that it is difficult to do the finest quality of planing feeding at a high speed. The second had been a puzzle, until solved by the introduction of the segmented or sectional roll, probably by Baxter D. Whitney (Fig. 4-12). This increased the capacity of the planer several hundred percent.

Sectional rolls are especially featured on better machines (Figs. 4-13, 4-14, 4-15, 4-16) and much to be preferred since they adjust themselves to the shape of the lumber. When two or more pieces of different thicknesses are fed through at the same time, a sectional feed roll holds each one securely on the bed. This greatly protected against kickback which was common on old, solid-roll planers when a loosely held piece of lumber came into contact with the knives. A sectional chipbreaker is always used with such a feed roll.

The planer is often designed so when taking a heavy cut the raising of the infeed roll will also partially raise the chipbreaker so as to readily admit the lumber under the chipbreaker.

A sectional roll usually consists of corrugated rings notched internally. A smaller disk with matching prongs which looks like a spider is keyed to the arbor. Coil springs are pinched between the notches in the ring and the disk's prongs. In a sense, the ring floats on the disk. When a board is fed into the machine it forces the ring upward and the notches and prongs continue to make direct contact and work against each other.

Each spring-loaded, corrugated segment has an independent movement. This yield can vary from 5/16" to 3/4". Therefore the infeed roll adapts itself to variations in thickness of glued-up lumber or very rough and uneven boards. Furthermore, when a board is placed between the rolls, a spring mechanism permits the entire roll to lift as much as 1" on some machines.

Whitney's sectional rolls were made up of fluted sections that yielded independently of each other and conformed to the unevenness of the material being planed. The tension in each section was obtained from coil springs acting at right angles to steel wings which were a part of the roll shaft.

The drive was against the shoulders of the sections and not against the springs, giving to each section a steady and positive drive. Each section exercised a uniform pressure on the material being planed. All the sections were central to the roll arbor on which they were mounted when the roll was not feeding.

Whitney sectional rolls would adapt themselves to the irregularities of glued-up or narrow stock with less liability of breaking the material than any other type. They would feed as many narrow strips as the planer bed could hold, giving to each strip a steady rate of feed.

However, even with sectional rolls, the thickest pieces going through the machine are acted upon more powerfully.

On Crescent Machine Co.'s 1924 26 x 8-inch Planer (Fig. 4-17) each section of the roll was 1" wide and designed so that the pressure spring was located outside of it. This simplified the construction of the roll and rendered it more efficient in operation since each individual section had separate adjustment where it was easy to get at and if for any reason one of the springs failed to function, proper adjustment could be made or the spring replaced without tearing down the entire feed roll.

J. A. Fay & Egan Co.'s No. 19 Improved Extra Heavy Planer And Smoother (Fig. 2-63) had feed rolls furnished with sectional weights so that the lightest or heaviest pressure could be readily given. The weight arms were also fitted with springs forming a cushion to the weights and acted instead of the weights when taking a thin cut, a great advantage in surfacing thin lumber.

On older machines the infeed roll is often held down by heavy cast-iron weights which can be adjusted in or out along pivoted arms to decrease or increase the pressure on the roll. The roll's own weight, plus the force from the springs or weights, holds the wood down but at the same time allows it to rise to accommodate a large variation in thickness.

However, the upper rolls on J. A. Fay & Co.'s Yankee Cylinder Planing Machine (Fig. 2-2) were furnished with Goodyear's Patent Rubber Machine Springs, by which the pressure could be readily adjusted. Richardson, Meriam & Co.'s No. 0 Small Cylinder Planing Machine (Fig. 1-9) had feeds rolls fitted with rubber springs or with weights and rubber springs combined. The outfeed roll on H. B. Smith Machine Co.'s 1887 New Surface Planing Machine (Fig. 4-18) was held down by rubber springs and the infeed by adjustable weights.

The use of a steel spring compression system (Fig. 4-19) eliminated entirely the slow acting and cumbersome levers and weights. This system furnished a uniform pressure at all times and adjusted automatically according to the unevenness of stock being fed.

On some machines like Rowley & Hermance Co.'s "Peacemaker" Double Belted Single Surfacer (Fig. 2-24) the weights for the upper infeed roll were connected with improved compensating levers which forced the roll to raise parallel at all times, so equal pressure was applied on the lumber the entire width of the machine. This gave a perfectly horizontal lift and prevented twisting the gearing.

Williamsport Machine Co.'s 1898 No. 3 Single Surfacer (Fig. 4-20) and its New And Improved Surface Planer (Fig. 4-21) had weighted infeed rolls joined by rocker shaft connections. This made it impossible for one end of the roll to raise and the other end to stay down, thus allowing the feed roll to press only on one edge of the stock, as was the case with most planers where the weights and levers were not connected with a rocker shaft. The outfeed roll received its tension from steel coil springs.

On the author's John A. White Co. planer, the infeed and outfeed rolls are connected on each side by a pair of pivoted yokes with adjustable heavy weights and work as a unit. The infeed roll is designed to open further than the outfeed roll.

On American Wood Working Machine Co.'s No. 1 Single Surfacer (Fig. 2-40) pressure on the upper infeed roll was obtained by adjustable spring tension attached to an equalizer bar. However, a foot treadle was also provided for temporarily increasing the pressure at will. The company's 1923 No. 5 Single Surfacer (Fig. 4-22) likewise had a foot treadle. Northfield Foundry & Machine Co.'s very similar 1923 No. 5 Single Surfacer (Fig. 4-23) featured a foot pedal for extra pressure. Crescent Machine Co.'s 1916 26 x 8-inch Planer (Fig. 4-24) had two foot levers. On P. B. Yates Machine Co.'s 1917 No. 156 Cabinet Planer (Fig. 4-25), No. 151 Single Surfacer (Fig. 4-26) and No. 5 Planer (Fig. 4-27), extra pressure could be brought to bear on the infeed roll by means of a foot lever on either side of the infeed end.

On Baxter D. Whitney & Son's 1930 No. 29 (Fig. 4-28) and No. 32 Single Surfacers (Fig. 4-29) additional pressure could be instantly applied to the roll by foot pressure on the levers at machine's front.

CHIPBREAKER

With very few exceptions, all planers have a chipbreaker set closely in front of the cutterhead serving several purposes. Its functions are to hold the lumber firmly against the bed limiting the cut to produce an accurate thickness, to break the shavings or chips into smaller pieces, to lessen the bounce of thinner boards, and to direct the flow of chips out of the planer. It also minimizes gouged ends or snipes (long dished-out circular grooves) on the board's ends as it enters or leaves the cutting zone.

The main purpose of the chipbreaker is to prevent the grain from tearing up when the cutterhead knives strike the board. It helps control splintering ahead of the knives by holding down the wood in front of the cutting edge, preventing it from continuing into the wood in front of the knives. It moves concentrically with the cutterhead.

The chips lifted by the chisel-like action of the knives are also prevented from digging in along the grain and becoming long splinters by the shape and configuration of the cutterhead itself, which, like the cap on a hand plane, causes the partly severed chip to crack and bend back on itself. If there were no chipbreaker, lumber would tend to tear or split off in long slivers. Very early planers relied on the cutterhead design alone.

The chipbreaker is basically a curved, one-piece metal bar with a flat base which swings concentric with the cutterhead and presses the work piece against the bed before it reaches the knives. Both the chipbreaker and the pressure bar move in an arc rather than actually moving straight up and down. This keeps them very close to the cutting zone.

Chipbreakers are usually designed to rise along with the infeed roll. Some early machines used a roll for a hold down and had a separate pressure from the shavings-guard, which also served as the chipbreaker.

Many models like Defiance Machine Works' 26" Patent Four-Roll Surface Planer (Fig. 2-1) were designed so the chipbreaker and pressure bar moved in a true circle with the knives in order to remain the same distance from the knives when taking a light or heavy cut, essential for smooth planing. The planer's chipbreaker and pressure bar were also hinged at their rear ends, so that they could be lifted back out of the way, giving easy access to the knives when re-sharpening was necessary.

Because unmachined or flat shoe surfaces on some planers caused harmful drag, some manufacturers like Boice-Crane Co. chose to have arc-shaped shoe surfaces on their chipbreakers and pressure bars, accurately milled to ensure absolute contact throughout the width of the work piece (Fig. 2-12).

On early machines and cheaper models, the chipbreaker is simply an adjustable solid metal bar resting on the lumber which only allows feeding one board at a time. In more sophisticated machines the bar, like the upper infeed roll, is divided into several sections with heavy compression springs or weights above each, permitting each section to conform individually to uneven or varying lumber thicknesses allowing multiple board planing.

On Crescent Machine Co.'s 1924 26 x 8-inch Planer, each unit of the chipbreaker was 2" wide with the pressure springs on the outside where they were easy to get at (Fig. 4-30). The winged thumb nut at the top of the tension screw provided for very quick and efficient adjustment to ensure the proper amount of pressure at all times. When one or more of the individual sections had moved upward to the limit of its flexibility (1/4"), the entire bar supporting all of the adjustable sections raised up and after the thicker piece had past through the machine, it would drop back, and the different sections would again automatically function as separate units.

On older machines, adjustable weights on levers pressed the solid chipbreaker down on the wood. As early as 1880 a few were using rubber blocks on the chipbreaker as well as for the pressure bar. The chipbreaker must always rest on the material while it is running through the machine. When the material is fed through, it should raise about 1/32". Its own weight plus the force from the springs holds the wood down, but at the same time it has to lift as a unit as much as the sectional infeed roll.

Baxter D. Whitney Co. began using chipbreakers made of cast iron fitted with a flexible spring extending the whole length of its lower edge as early as 1898 (Fig. 4-31). The spring brought the weight of the chipbreaker down on the stock being planed. Since the edge was flexible it fit into all surface irregularities and pressed the lumber firmly to the bed. When occasional, unusually large humps or ridges in the lumber bent the spring unduly at any point, it bent around, the fingers projecting from the back of the chipbreaker until the chipbreaker itself rested on the stock, preventing breaking of the spring and interference with the knives. The chipbreaker was entirely automatic and pressed the stock at a line which was always the same distance from the knives whether the cut was heavy or light. The chipbreaker shoe could be reversed end for end, when one edge was worn down.

The chipbreaker on J.A. Fay & Egan Co.'s No. 19 Improved Extra Heavy Planer And Smoother (Fig. 2-63) was fitted with a spring-steel shoe (lip). It always swung concentric, following the path of the knives closely, whether taking a light or heavy cut.

American Wood Working Machine Co.'s 1909 No. 4 1/2 Single Surface Planer (Fig. 2-39) could be purchased with a solid chipbreaker, one divided into four sections, or sectional with 2" independent sections, or with an elastic steel lip (spring) close to the cut (Fig. 4-32).

The chipbreaker on Fay & Egan's 1910 No. 156 New Cabinet Smoothing Planer (Fig. 4-33) rose concentric with the circle of the knives, always resting on the board equidistant from the edge of the cut. At the lower edge of the bar was a spring extending from end to end, which rested on the stock instead of the bar proper. This spring was strong enough, in itself, to press out all ordinary crooks of a board and to hold it firmly upon the table.

The chipbreaker on Oliver Machinery Co.'s ca. 1921 No. 61 Single Four Roll Double Belted Surfacer had a steel spring shoe secured to the lower part which not only held the stock firmly on the bed, but also yielded to any ordinary inequalities in rough stock (Fig. 2-47). An adjustable weight regulated the pressure.

The flexible chipbreaker on Greenlee Brothers & Co.'s ca. 1944 No. 110 Six-Roll Single Planer (Fig. 4-34) had its spring slotted to equalize the pressure at all points and was reversible so that it could be used until both edges were worn out. The method of holding was designed so that the bending did not take place along a line through the middle only. The entire spring was flexible across the width from edge to edge, greatly increasing the useful life of the spring.

CUTTERHEAD

Cutterheads, sometimes called cylinders in old literature, cut in the up-milling direction, the knives revolving at high speed in the opposite direction from that in which the board is moving, the feed and cutterhead working against each other. The knives, which are mounted in the rotating cutterhead, travel in a circular path around the head. Each knife strikes the lumber diagonally and, like a chisel, splits and breaks away a sliver forming a small arc shaped cut.

Cutterheads can be square, triangular, or round (Fig. 4-35). Usually the number of knives varies from two to four, but they can have as many as four, six, or more knives according to their size. The round cutterhead was introduced into the U.S. by the Oliver Machinery Co. in 1908. The company would also custom machine a safety head to fit another manufacturer's machine—any diameter, any length, etc.

The presence of a square cutterhead does not always indicate an early age. Such heads continued to be offered (usually as options) well into the 1920s and 1930s (Figs. 4-36 & 4-37).

Cutterhead diameter depends on the number of knives used. Eight to 16-knife planers require cutting circles from 9" to 12" in diameter. Large cutting circles improve surface quality but the requirement of compact planer designs and the difficulty of handling lumber at speeds much above 1,000 fpm has pretty much limited cutterhead diameters to about 12".

Modern cutterheads run in precision ball bearings and many are motor driven. In the latter case the end of the cutterhead is the rotor of the motor on some machines. On others the motor is mounted on a bracket bolted to the frame and is connected to the cutterhead with a coupling or belt (Fig. 4-38). On early planers, the cutterhead was rotated by flat belts connected to a countershaft with tight and loose pulleys so the machine could be "turned off" (Fig. 4-39). The countershaft, in turn, received its power from the shop's main line shaft.

Cutterheads are designed so that the knives are set at an exact angle to the head called the cutting angle. The angle the ground knife edge makes with the wood on contact is called the clearance angle.

Cutterhead speed is commonly fixed at 3,600 rpm since this is the speed of the motor usually mounted directly on the spindle; further, 3,600 rpm is the highest speed at which knives can be consistently jointed so each cuts equally. Modern vee-belt-driven cutterheads commonly run at 3,500 to 5,000 rpm.

The method of holding the knives firmly in place varies. On newer planers, the wedge bar lock is most prevalent. The knife and a steel block drop into a dovetail groove machined in the cutterhead and are held in place by screws which, when turned out, wedge or clamp the knife in position.

On older cutterheads, the slab method may be used (Fig. 4-40). Here the head is made in three parts with two caps or slabs bolted onto it with recessed bolts to hold the knife in place.

PRESSURE BAR

Immediately behind the cutterhead is a heavy iron casting with a hardened steel lip called the pressure bar which rides on the surface just planed and forms an upper limiting stop (Figs. 4-41). It holds the wood firmly flat on the table so the knives will not dig into the end of the board as it passes below the cutterhead and throughout the remainder of the cut. The bar also keeps the end of the board from tipping up as it leaves the cutting zone, thereby helping to prevent the clip or snipe on the board's end.

A pressure bar is now common to all quality planers. A patent was issued to J. P. Woodbury in 1873, broadly covering a rotary cutterhead combined with a yielding pressure bar to hold lumber down against the lifting action of the knives. Like the Woodworth patent, it too caused litigation.

Because it rides on the planed surface of a board, it is never made sectional. Though resembling the chipbreaker, it is far more rigid. It is adjustable for height and usually is held down by adjustable heavy coil springs so that its own weight, plus the force from the springs, holds the wood down but at the same time allows it to rise slightly to accommodate a slight variation in thickness.

Almost all problems can be traced to a misaligned pressure bar. The tension must be heavy but also must allow the wood to pass through without binding. The lower surface is adjusted parallel to the bed and tangent to the cutting circle. Some designs feature a quick-release mechanism to assist in clearing jams or breakups in the machine.

On early designs it was stationary, some manufacturers claiming a yielding bar produced waves on the surface. On others, it rose and fell beneath adjustable rubber compression springs.

OUTFEED ROLL

This roll moves in the same direction as the front roll and in unison with it. The outfeed roll is usually of smooth, one-piece construction to help avoid marring the finished surface of the material after leaving the cutterhead. Some have micro fine grooves milled along their surface, others a rubber coating—all intended to improve the grip on the lumber but without marring it. Set slightly lower than the infeed roller, its function is to continue feeding the material through the machine after it leaves the infeed roll and push it clear of machine. It is often provided with a thin steel wiper or other device, which scrapes off any shavings or pitch that might adhere to it (Fig. 4-42). If allowed to accumulate there, shavings would mar the finished surface of a board.

TABLE ROLLS

The table rolls, also of smooth, one-piece construction, cut down the friction of the material on the table caused by the downward pressure from the rollers, chipbreaker, and pressure bar above. The rougher the material, the higher the rolls are set to lessen friction on the bed itself. Rough material feeds harder. One is usually located directly beneath each feed roll. Typically these are idler rolls, but production models often feature powered bed rolls.

A few early manufacturers used a large idler roll directly under the knife to relieve the friction due to the downward pressure of the cut. This was opposed by some of the best builders, on the grounds that the board bent over the roll if it projected far enough to be of any real use and the work would not be true.

That this pressure downward is considerable is evident by the fact that tables are apt to wear hollow at that point. Some machines, as stated earlier, had a false plate below the cutterhead which could be replaced or re-machined. Often a strip of steel was set into the table at that point.

Some planers also have idler rolls placed at each end of the table to reduce friction in feeding heavy timbers (Fig. 4-43).

J.A. Fay & Egan Co.'s No. 3 Heavy Planer And Smoother (Fig. 4-39) had four large gear-powered feed rolls. The two geared rolls in the bed being larger than the upper ones was supposed to prevent all clipping of the ends of boards or gouging out, a fault possessed by many machines.

PROCESS OF PLANING

As lumber is pushed forward on the table, the first thing to act on it is the corrugated feed roll which pulls it into the machine. This roll, like the smooth outfeed roll, is held down by weights or by heavy springs attached to each end of the roll.

After leaving this roll, the lumber proceeds a few inches and then comes in contact with the chipbreaker, which rides on top of it and bears down on it heavily, directly in front of the cutterhead. The chipbreaker serves the planer knives just as the chipbreaker or cap-iron serves the hand plane. It is held down on the lumber by weights or springs and is designed to move concentric to the knives and cutterhead.

Just after passing the chipbreaker, the board comes in contact with the knives of the cutterhead, which revolves at high speed in the opposite direction from that in which the board is moving. These knives plane the upper surface of the board smooth and to uniform thickness.

The shavings are thrown out with great force from the space between the cutterhead and the chipbreaker. These are usually exhausted through a galvanized iron hood fitting over the cutterhead. Suction is created in the hood and pipes connected to it by means of a motor-driven blower.

Leaving the knives, the lumber passes under the pressure bar directly behind the cutterhead which rides on the newly planed surface and holds the board firmly down on the bed while the knives continue to do their work. This prevents chattering and irregular cutting. It is regulated by springs and adjusted so that the lumber as it leaves the knives can pass accurately underneath it. On some machines the distance between pressure bar and chipbreaker is as little as 1 1/8".

The lumber next passes beneath the smooth outfeed or delivery roll, designed to continue to pull the board through the machine after its end has cleared the grip of the infeed roll.

BASIC ADJUSTMENTS

Based on an examination of dozens of planer manuals ranging from small 12" models to 24" models, the general rule of thumb is: solid infeed rolls should be set 1/32" below the cutterhead's arc (the knife's lowest point) and 1/16" with sectional rolls; the chipbreaker should be set at 1/32" below the cutterhead's arc; the pressure bar at .000"; the outfeed roll at 1/32" below; and the bed rolls .003" above the bed when planing smooth lumber and at .015" for rough-sawn lumber.

The beds on some planers like the Buss No. 208 have their front and rear sections machined or set lower than the center section, since they are intended to only help support lumber. This can be as much as 1/64". To work around this, use only the center section as your reference point.

A planer can easily produce work accurate to thousandths of an inch. To achieve this accuracy pay attention to adjustments, alignment procedures, and preventive maintenance.

GAGE BLOCK

A simple, inexpensive dial indicator with a magnetic base will yield precise readouts when adjusting the machine. However, if you do not have or know how to use a dial indicator, a simple shop-made gage block (Fig. 4-44) will serve just as well.

The hardwood block's dimensions are relative, but its legs must span the width of the bed roll and rest securely on the bed on either side. Some operators use two wooden straight edges about 1 1/2 x 4 x 48-inches which are rested on the bed rolls after they have been set.

Using the block will require shims or feeler gages of 1/16" and 1/32" thickness. If the exact thicknesses are unavailable, their approximate decimal equivalents are: 1/16"=.060"; 1/32"=.030".

SECTION *thru No. 105 Planer showing 4-knife cutterhead, location and mounting of rolls, chipbreaker, back pressure bar and grinder bar.*

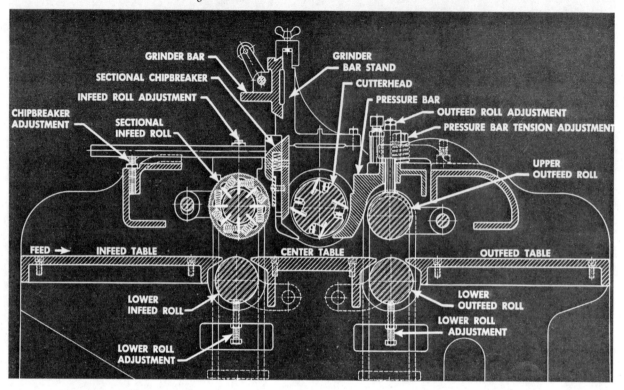

Fig. 4-1: Section Drawing Through No. 105 Surfacer Showing Feeding System. Baxter D. Whitney & Son Co. Circa 1930s Brochure.

No. 110 Planer arranged for Belt Drive. Note that the Pulley Housing is adjustable for belting from any direction.

Fig. 4-2: No. 110 Six-Roll Single Planer. Greenlee Bros. & Co., Circa 1944 Catalog.

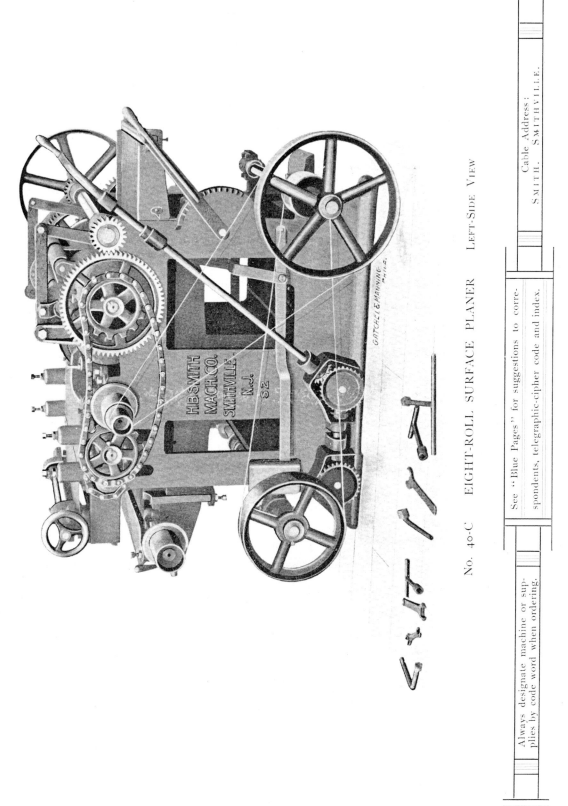

No. 40-C   EIGHT-ROLL SURFACE PLANER   LEFT-SIDE VIEW

Always designate machine or supplies by code word when ordering.	See "Blue Pages" for suggestions to correspondents, telegraphic-cipher code and index.	Cable Address: SMITH. SMITHVILLE.

Fig. 4-3: No. 40-C Eight Roll Surface Planing Machine. Single Or Double. H. B. Smith Machine Co., 1902 55th Ed. Catalog.

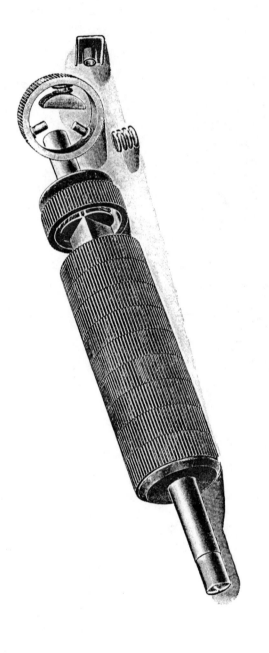

SECTIONAL ROLL.

Triple, continuous, uniform drive. Each section, 6 inches diameter by 2 inches face, is automatically adjustable to limited variations in thicknesses of stock. The whole, weighted and driven as one roll, is applicable to our Nos. 153 and 173.

Length of Roll, or width of Machine	24 in.	27 in.	30 in.	36 in.
Code Word, corrugated	Pace	Pacer	Pack	Packer
Code Word, smooth	Paco	Pacos	Pact	Paction

Fig. 4-4: Sectional Roll. Berlin Machine Works, Catalogue Series E. Circa 1897.

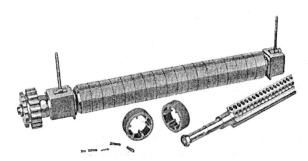

Top Infeed Roll showing ball end on the bearing cap for expansion linkage. Note the double Timken bearings at each end. Steel sections are 2″ wide and have chamfered corners. Shaft is milled from solid steel bar. Section springs are mounted on pins and sleeves to prevent distortion. The roll sections and the spline roll shafts are hardened to reduce wear.

Pressure Bar   An independent adjustment at each end of the exceptionally heavy pressure bar provides for leveling it parallel to the cut. A separate single hand-wheel, graduated to one thousandth of an inch, makes the adjustment for height. Therefore, when the bar is raised or lowered the parallel adjustment is not affected. The lower edge is provided with a hardened steel, replaceable wearing strip. Ample spring pressure, a simplicity of adjustment, and rigid heavy construction with the edge of the lip working very close to the cut keeps the stock on the platen and helps to eliminate chatter and "sniping." Pieces as short as four inches can be run successfully, if they are kept butted.

Platen   The platen consists of a thick, hardened steel plate, accurately ground to a mirror finish and securely bolted in a deep-ribbed heavy cast-iron sub-platen. The latter is bolted to substantial brackets cast on the bed. The steel platen can be shimmed up for regrinding when this is eventually necessary, or it can be easily replaced with a new one if desirable.

Feed Rolls   Four Timken roller bearings are provided on each feed roll, two at each end mounted in semi-self-aligning boxes. The bottom rolls and the top out-feed roll are of iron cast to heavy

steel shafts in such a manner that they can never come loose. The internal shape is such as to resist bending stresses, and the rolls and shaft ends are accurately ground. The bottom roll bearing cases are seated on wedges, with the adjustment brought within easy reach from outside the machine. Only one wrench is necessary as the adjustments have spring locks.

The top out-feed roll is carried by the top out girt, and the spring pressure sleeves and supporting studs project upward through the girt so they can be adjusted from outside the machine. The top in-feed rolls can also be furnished in the solid type, either smooth or corrugated. They are supported by studs projecting from the top in-feed girt with the adjusting nuts above the girt. A rubber cushion absorbs the shock when the rolls drop behind the stock. Even pressure is applied by long springs through an equalizing bar and convenient handwheels above the girt. All the top roll bearing cases are guided in pockets machined in the side frames, so that correct alignment is always maintained.

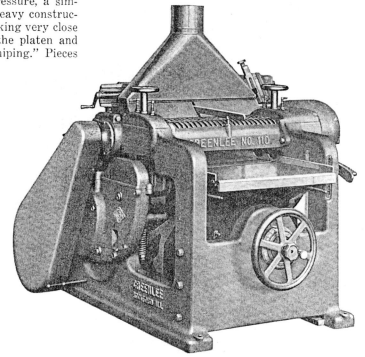

View from Gear Case Side of No. 110 Planer with Belted Feed Drive. Photograph also shows Dust Hood in place.

[5]

Fig. 4-5: No. 110 Six-Roll Single Planer. Sectional Roll & Bearing Boxes. Greenlee Bros. & Co., Circa 1944 Catalog.

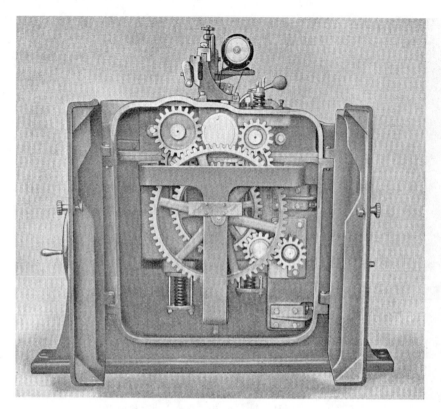

RIGHT SIDE — Shows accessibility of gearing and simplicity of design. All gears on one side of planer and fully protected.

Fig. 4-6: No. 105. Right Side Showing gearing. Baxter D. Whitney & Son Co. Circa 1930s Brochure.

Fig. 4-7: Chain & Belt Drive. No. 208 20 x 8 Planer. Buss Machine Works. Circa 1950. Author's Collection.

Fig. 4-8: No. 52-C Surface Planing Machine Single. Available As 24 & 26 x 8. Driven By Chain From Top Infeed Roll With A Scraper. H. B. Smith Machine Co., 1902 55th Ed. Catalog.

Fig. 4-9: Belt Drive From Cutterhead. 24 x 8 Planer. John A. White Co. Circa 1876. Author's Collection.

WHITNEY No. 37 ELECTRIC SINGLE PLANER

Fig. 4-10: No. 37 Six Feed Roll, Heavy Duty Single Planer, Electric Or Belt Driven. Baxter D. Whitney & Son Co. 1930s Brochure.

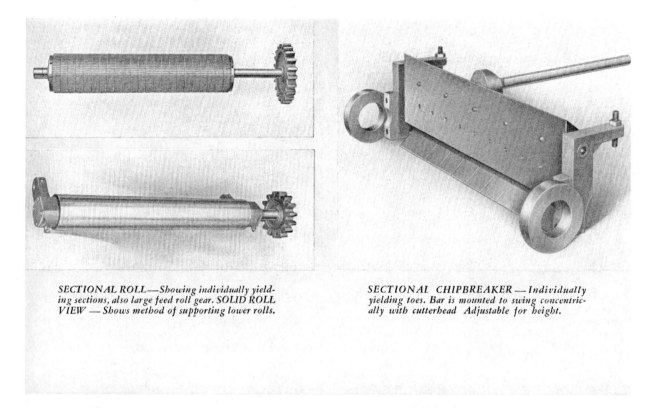

SECTIONAL ROLL—Showing individually yielding sections, also large feed roll gear. SOLID ROLL VIEW — Shows method of supporting lower rolls.

SECTIONAL CHIPBREAKER — Individually yielding toes. Bar is mounted to swing concentrically with cutterhead Adjustable for height.

FEEDS

- Micro-feed Selector, operated by convenient handwheel at left front of machine, gives any feed desired between 20 and 60 feet per minute

- Actual rate of feed is shown on dial indicator under operating conditions

CHIPBREAKER

- SECTIONAL CHIPBREAKER of new and improved design. 2¼″ wide sections, spring loaded, yield independently for holding uneven or glued-up stock or separate pieces

- Bar swings concentric with cutterhead. Has convenient adjustment for height

- Holds stock firmly, close to cutterhead

4-KNIFE ROUND CUTTERHEAD — Motor rotor is mounted directly on cutterhead arbor. Note large housings for over-size cutterhead bearings.

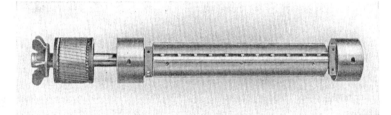

Fig. 4-11: No. 105. Sectional Roll, Solid Roll, And Sectional Chipbreaker. Baxter D. Whitney & Son Co. Circa 1930s Brochure.

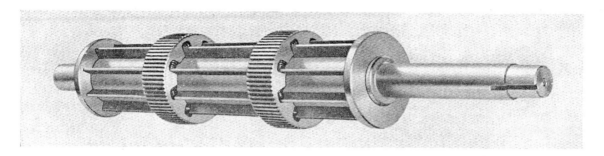

Sectional top infeed roll showing construction and two of the fluted sections and springs.

Fig. 4-12: No. 29A & 32A Single Surface Planers. Sectional Roll. Baxter D. Whitney & Son Co. 1930s Brochure.

Fig. 4-13: Sectional Roll And Chipbreaker. American Wood Working Machine Co., 10th Ed. Catalog, 1915.

26 x 8-Inch Crescent Planer

Variable Feed
(Patented)

THIS planer is suitable for use where a substantial, dependable machine is required for continuous operation on accurate and heavy work. (Fig. 202 and 203). While it is neat in design, it is heavily built and being very compact requires a small amount of floor space. At the same time, it will handle lumber of large dimensions. The machine has four power driven feed rolls and has flanged pulley on each end of the head for two drive belts.

Pressure. Any amount of pressure up to 600 pounds on the upper in-feeding roll is provided by means of two springs controlled by two small hand wheels. Two foot levers make it possible to obtain additional pressure, momentarily, when wanted. The springs are flexible, act quickly and do not give the pounding strains that are common with weights. A trial will show the superiority of this construction; but any purchaser who should consider it undesirable after trial, will be furnished with weights in place of the springs, free of cost.

The Head is furnished with two knives, but a four sided square head may be furnished when so ordered, the only extra charge being for two additional knives. Round safety head fitted with four knives may be supplied at an additional price when ordered.

The Countershaft may be placed on the ceiling above the machine, on the floor back of the machine or below the floor.

Sectional Feed Roll and Sectional Chip Breaker (Fig. 319 and 319-A) with sufficient adjustment to take care of lumber varying ¼ inch in thickness can be furnished at an additional price. Each section of the feed roll is 1 inch wide and is so designed that the pressure spring is located outside of it. This simplifies the construction of the roll and renders it more efficient in operation as each individual section has separate adjustment where it is easy to get at and if for any reason one of the springs should fail to function, proper adjustment may be made or the spring replaced without the necessity of tearing down the entire feed roll. When considering a planer with a sectional feed roll this feature should not be overlooked.

Each unit of the sectional chip breaker is 2 inches in width with the pressure springs on the outside where they are easy to get at. The winged thumb nut at the top of the tension screw provides for a

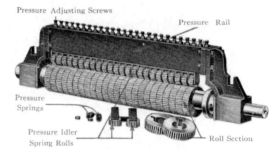

Fig. 319—Sectional Feed Roll
Patent Applied for

very quick and efficient adjustment to insure the proper amount of pressure at all times. When one or more of the individual sections has moved upward to the limit of its flexibility which is ¼ inch, then the bar that supports all of the adjustable sections raises upward and after the thicker piece has passed through the machine, the different sections of the chip breaker will again automatically

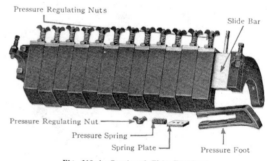

Fig. 319-A—Sectional Chip Breaker
Patent Applied for

function as separate units. The sectional chip breaker is very efficient in operation and is always furnished when the sectional feed roll is ordered.

Feed. The machine is furnished only with variable friction feed and will surface at any rate of feed from 15 to 60 feet per minute.

Fig. 4-14: Sectional Infeed & Chipbreaker. Crescent Machine Co., Aug. 25, 1924 Brochure.

This drawing shows a cross section of the machine, with a hand pointing to the sectional roll, a description of which follows:

Cross Section Sectional Roll and Chip-Breaker

A is the spur driver which extends the entire length of roll, and is driven by gearing on the machine. *B* are the roll shells driven by *A*. These shells are 3 inches wide and set closely to one another. *C* is a weighting roll which rests on the top of *B*. *D* is a weight which saddles on *C* with its fulcrum at *F*. *E* is an equalizing rock-bar with bearings between each weight *D*, which swings on shaft *G*. *H* is the yoke cover over sectional roll and contains bearings for shaft *G*.

It will be seen that a narrow stick entering the rolls will only engage as many sections as its width covers, and they will raise with independent weights on each, independently of the balance of the sectional roll.

Each section can rise ⅜ of an inch independent of its neighbor, but if a piece has more than ⅜ of an inch variation, it will raise the spur *A*, which is also weighted and connected by roll boxes and links to rock-bar *E*. It will in turn raise these fulcrums, *F*, in the same relative position as to the other roll, and never varies their independent weight.

A short study of the cuts of this roll and chip breaker will give a clear idea of its action. We call particular attention to the fact, that this sectional roll has no springs at all, and has more independent action than any other sectional roll on the market.

Of the chip-breaker, *K* are the nose pieces which independently slide vertically on slide bar *J*, to an equal extent of that of the roll section. *J* is fulcrumed at *L*, and swings up around the head when the rise exceeds ⅝ of an inch. Each nose piece, *K*, has a spring and weight to force it down on the stock independent of its neighbor, and absolutely holds the same solidly to the bed while being worked.

pieces of the chip-breaker swing up and around the head, on a common center, they being governed by a one-piece slide-bar, to which they are attached.

Sectional Roll

This infeed end view of the sectional roll machine shows how it handles a number of narrow pieces, of different thicknesses, at one time. Also how each section of the chip-breaker acts on the stock, independent of its neighbor, and in conjunction with the section of the roll in front of it.

CHIP-BREAKER

SECTIONAL ROLL.

SECTIONAL ROLL AT REST.

Sectional Roll at Rest

A view of the sectional roll is shown here, with the machine bed dropped and the machine empty. It shows how each section has dropped to a common center, and how the entire roll presents a continuous working surface the same as would be presented by a solid roll.

Fig. 4-15: Divided Roll And Chipbreaker For Holding Lumber Of Two Different Thicknesses. Sectional feed roll Using. No Internal Springs. H. B. Smith Machine Co., 1902 55th Ed. Catalog.

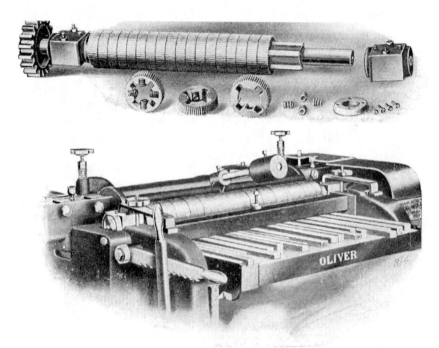

VIEWS OF SECTIONAL FEED ROLL
Note the Positive Drive and the Fool-Proof Construction.

Fig. 4-16: No. 61 Four Roll Cabinet Planer. Double Belted. Section Rolls.
Oliver Machinery Co. Catalog No. 21, Circa 1920.

26x8-Inch Crescent Planer, Four Rolls Driven, Variable Feed

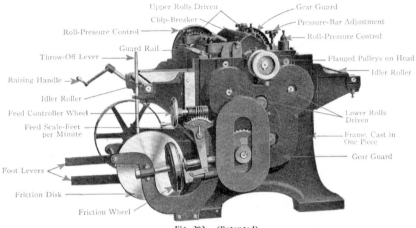

Fig. 202   (Patented)

Dimensions

Width and thickness will plane, inches	26x8
Width of drive belts, inches	4
Diameter of pulleys on head, inches	5
Size of tight and loose pulleys, inches	10x6
Size of drive pulleys on countershaft, inches	20x4
Speed of countershaft, per minute, revolutions	1000
Giving head a speed of per minute, revolutions	4000
Slowest feed per minute, feet	15
Fastest feed per minute, feet	60
Length of feed belt (2¼ inches wide)	8'4"
Length of table, inches	52
Shortest piece will feed through, inches	14
Rate of feed, per minute, feet	15 to 60
Diameter of upper feed rolls, inches	4
Diameter of lower feed rolls, inches	3¼
Floor space, exclusive of countershaft, inches	59x69
Horsepower required	10 to 15
Cubic measure, boxed for export, feet	110
Gross weight, boxed for export, pounds	3500
Domestic shipping weight, pounds	3000
Telegraphic code word	Meord
Telegraphic code word, safety head	Merda
Telegraphic code word, Sectional feed roll	Mandr
Telegraphic code word, Sectional chip breaker	Maeoj

Regular Equipment. Each machine is furnished with countershaft, with self oiling loose pulley, pair of two knives and two wrenches. (No belts furnished.)

26x8-Inch Crescent Planer, Variable Feed

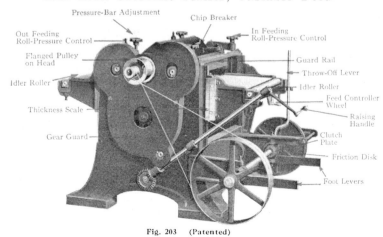

Fig. 203   (Patented)

Fig. 4-17: 26 x 8 Planer. Sectional Infeed & Chipbreaker. Crescent Machine Co., Aug. 25, 1924, Brochure.

New Surface Planing Machine.

Fig. 4-18: New Surface Planing Machine. 24 x 8 Pony Planer. Infeed Roll Corrugated & Held Down By Adjustable Weights. Outfeed Roll Held Down By Rubber Springs. Forged Steel Cutterhead. Two Knives. Binder For Starting Feed Also Provided With A Brake For Stopping Feed. Gears Guarded. H. B. Smith Machine Co., 1887 Catalog.

With Variable Feed and Direct-Attached Motor

Figure 7741

American No. 444 Single Finishing Planer

Fig. 4-19: No. 444 Single Finishing Planer. Available As 24, 30 & 36 x 7. Roll Shafts Held Down By Long Range Tempered Steel Springs Adjustable For Tension. Sectional Infeed & Chipbreaker. Each Section Carries Eight Tempered Tool Steel Springs 2 1/8". Sections And Drivers Are Of Hardened Steel. Feed Drive By Belts In The High Speed Portion Of The Transmission, Hardened Steel Roller Chains For The Intermediate, & Cut Gears For The Rolls Or Slow Portion. All Rolls Driven. American Wood Working Machine Co. Vocational Catalog 1920.

WILLIAMSPORT MACHINE CO.'S
No. 3, Single Surfacer.

Fig. 4-20: No. 3 Single Surfacer. 24 x 8. Double Belted. Solid Forged Steel Cutterhead. Front Roll Weighted & Connected With Rock Shaft, Making The Feed Roll Raise Parallel At All Times. "This will be found a great improvement over the old way of weighting feed rolls." Williamsport Machine Co., American Wood Working Machine Co. First Edition Catalog 1898.

WILLIAMSPORT MACHINE CO.'S

New and Improved Surface Planer.

Fig. 4-21: New And Improved Surface Planer. With Rocker Shaft. One Piece Cast Bed. Williamsport Machine Co., American Wood Working Machine Co. First Edition Catalog, 1898.

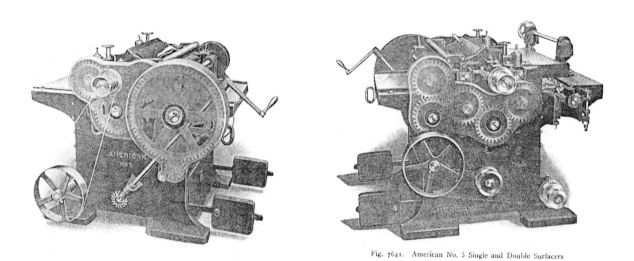

Fig. 7641. American No. 5 Single and Double Surfacers

Fig. 4-22: No. 5 Single Surfacer. American Wood Working Machine Co., Ninth Ed. Catalog, Circa 1909.

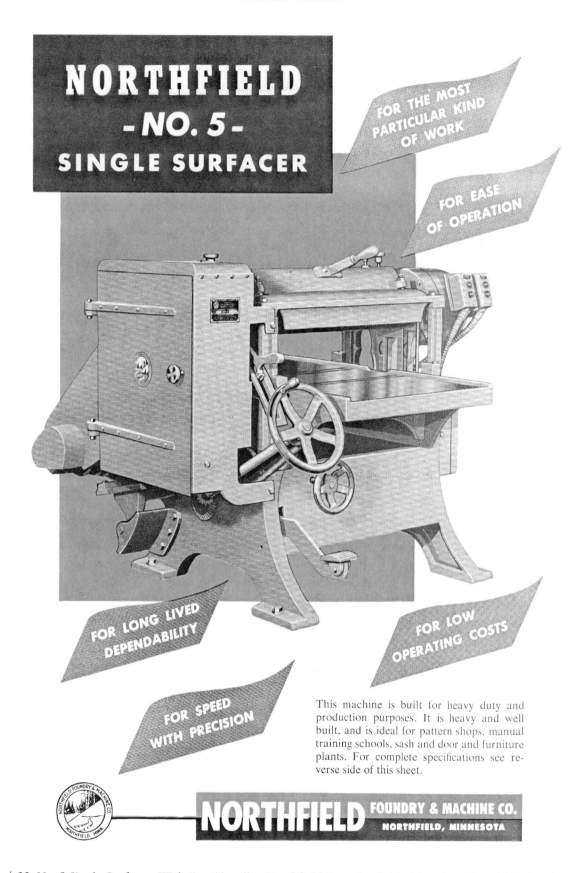

NORTHFIELD
-NO. 5-
SINGLE SURFACER

FOR THE MOST PARTICULAR KIND OF WORK

FOR EASE OF OPERATION

FOR LONG LIVED DEPENDABILITY

FOR LOW OPERATING COSTS

FOR SPEED WITH PRECISION

This machine is built for heavy duty and production purposes. It is heavy and well built, and is ideal for pattern shops, manual training schools, sash and door and furniture plants. For complete specifications see reverse side of this sheet.

NORTHFIELD FOUNDRY & MACHINE CO.
NORTHFIELD, MINNESOTA

Fig. 4-23: No. 5 Single Surfacer. With Foot Treadle. Northfield Foundry & Machine Co., Circa 1950 Brochure.

26-Inch Crescent Surfacer, Four Rolls Driven, Variable Feed

Fig. 4-24: 26 x 8 Planer. Variable Feed. Crescent Machine Co. Catalog, 1916.

YATES No. 156 CABINET SINGLE SURFACER
WITH EITHER DIRECT CONNECTED MOTOR OR BELT DRIVE
(See Description on Reverse Side)

P. B. Yates Machine Company
BELOIT, WISCONSIN, U.S.A.

Canadian Plant, with Offices, Hamilton, Ont.

Fig. 4-25: No. 156 Cabinet Single Surfacer. With Foot Treadle. P. B. Yates Machine Co. Dec. 1, 1917, Brochure.

YATES No. 151 SINGLE SURFACER

BUILT WITH or WITHOUT HOPPER FEED

(See Description on Reverse Side)

P.B.Yates Machine Company

BELOIT, WISCONSIN, U.S.A.

Canadian Plant, with Offices, Hamilton, Ont.

Fig. 4-26: No. 151 Single Surfacer. With Foot Treadle. P.B.Yates Machine Co. Jan. 15, 1918, Brochure.

| YATES-AMERICAN | MACHINE COMPANY |

No. 5 Single Surfacer

YATES-AMERICAN No. 5 Single Surfacer is designed for general work in planing mills and job factories. It is built either as a belt or motor driven machine. It will surface up to 24″ in width and to 8″ in thickness. The construction of the No. 5 is exceedingly durable throughout and the machine can be depended upon for good results and long service.

Regular Equipment

Head—4-knife square, 5″ cutting circle, $4\frac{13}{16}$″ swing. Pulley $4\frac{1}{2}$″ diameter, $4\frac{1}{2}$″ face. 4000 R. P. M., 2 knives, 38 degrees, furnished for head.

Drive—Tight and loose pulley 12″x6″. Countershaft $1\frac{11}{16}$″ diameter, 900 R. P. M.

Rolls—4, All driven, two top and two bottom, 4″ diameter. First upper roll corrugated, other smooth. Spring loaded. Bottom rolls smooth, adjustable.

Feeds—22 and 35 feet per minute.

Chipbreaker—Solid.

Stock—Thinnest $\frac{1}{16}$″. Shortest 13″. Shortest when butted 6″.

Hood—Size piping required 6″. (Outside dimension.)

H. P.—10.

Extra Equipment

CODE

Eagsl Round heads.

Ceand Setter and jointer.

Caevj Sectional roll and chipbreaker.

Caerf Ball Bearings.

Ceakz Motor knife grinder.

Cauxp Standard motor base and pulley for belt connection.

Cayax Motor mounted directly on cylinder. (Ball bearings and 3-knife round cylinder included.)

Code	Size	Floor Space	Wght. Lbs.	Boxed for Export Wght. Lbs.	Boxed for Export Cubic Feet
Afhuz	24″x8″	5′4″x4′11″	2700	3250	100

No. 1½ Single Surfacer

YATES-AMERICAN No. $1\frac{1}{2}$ Single Surfacer is a cabinet planer designed for high quality work and is used widely in furniture, carriage, chair and carpenter shops and in manual training schools. It is a medium priced surfacer.

Regular Equipment

Head—4-knife square, 4000 R. P. M., $4\frac{3}{8}$″ cutting circle. 2 35° knives furnished. Bearings $1\frac{11}{16}$″ diameter, 8″ long.

Drive—Tight and loose pulley 10″x5¼″. Countershaft $1\frac{7}{16}$″ diameter, 800 R. P. M.

Rolls—4. Two top and two bottom. $3\frac{1}{2}$″ diameter. Top rolls solid, spring loaded driven. Bottom rolls solid, smooth, adjustable.

Feeds—18 and 32 feet per minute.

Hood—Not furnished. Size piping required 5″. (Outside dimension).

Chipbreaker—Solid swinging type.

Stock—Thickest 8″. Shortest 12″. Shortest when butted 6″. Thinnest $\frac{1}{16}$″.

H. P.—5 to $7\frac{1}{2}$.

Extra Equipment

CODE

Eagsl Round heads.

Ceand Jointer and setter.

Caevj Sectional roll and flexible chipbreaker.

Caerf Ball Bearings.

Ceakz Motor knife grinder.

Cayax Motor drive. (Motor mounted on cylinder. Ball bearings and 3-knife round cylinder included.)

Cauxp Standard motor base and pulley for belt connection.

Code	Size	Floor Space	Wght. Lbs.	Boxed for Export Wght. Lbs.	Boxed for Export Cubic Feet
Afibw	24″x8″	4′6″x4′10″	2300	3000	105

| BELOIT, WISCONSIN U.S.A. |

Fig. 4-27: No. 5 Single Surfacer. With Foot Treadle. Yates-American Machine Co., Circa 1932 First Ed. Catalog.

WHITNEY No. 29 ELECTRIC-DRIVEN SINGLE SURFACE PLANER
Built in 36″, 40″ and 44″ wide.   Planes stock ⅟₁₆″ to 7″ in thickness.
Equipped with a 4-speed Motor direct connected to the feed shaft to drive
the feed works.

Fig. 4-28: No. 29 Electric Driven Single Surface Planer. With Foot Treadle. Baxter D. Whitney & Son Co. Circa 1935 Brochure.

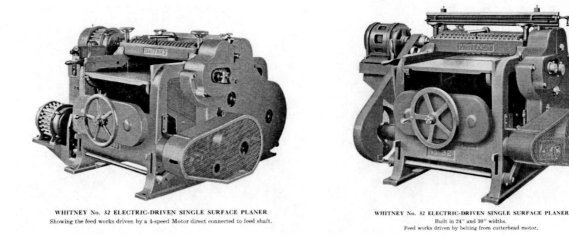

WHITNEY No. 32 ELECTRIC-DRIVEN SINGLE SURFACE PLANER
Showing the feed works driven by a 4-speed Motor direct connected to feed shaft.

WHITNEY No. 32 ELECTRIC-DRIVEN SINGLE SURFACE PLANER
Built in 24" and 30" widths.
Feed works driven by belting from cutterhead motor.

Fig. 4-29: No. 32 Electric Driven Single Surface Planer, Baxter D. Whitney & Son Co. No. 29 & 32 Single Surface Planers Brochure, Circa 1935, Original, Ex. Ills. p. 2

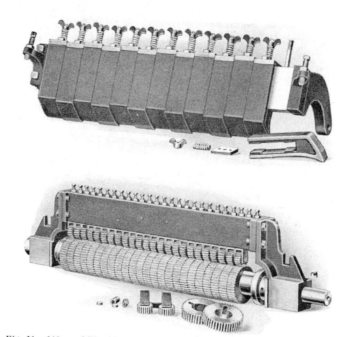

Fig. No. 319. and Fig. No. 319A. Sectional feed roll and sectional chip breaker may be supplied as extra equipment on the 26" x 8" Crescent Planer at a slight additional price.

Fig. 4-30: Sectional Infeed & Chipbreaker. Crescent Machine Co., 1930 Catalog.

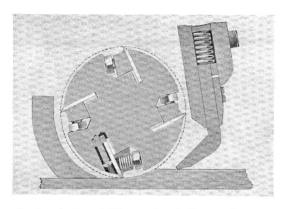

Sectional view of Whitney four-knife round cutter-head, sectional chipbreaker and close-action of pressure bar.

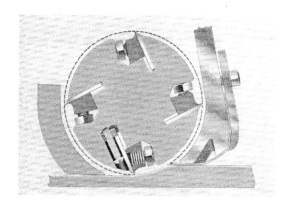

Whitney four-knife round cutterhead showing action of flexible chipbreaker and pad.

FOUR-KNIFE ROUND CUTTERHEAD

The No. 32A and No. 29A Planers are furnished with 4-knife round cutterheads with 5″ cutting circle, and thin high-speed steel knives. The cutterhead is made from alloy steel, heat treated, precision ground and accurately balanced. It is mounted in pre-loaded, precision ball bearings, sealed against dust and grit and lubricated by a Whitney developed oil lubrication system. Maximum cut for No. 32A Planer is $\frac{7}{8}$″; for No. 29A Planer, $\frac{3}{4}$″.

CHIPBREAKER

A sectional or flexible chipbreaker may be furnished.

SECTIONAL: Accommodates stock of uneven thickness, narrow pieces of varying thicknesses and glued-up stock. Holds stock firmly, close to cutterhead. Made up of individually yielding $2\frac{1}{4}$″ wide steel sections, spring loaded. Swings as a unit concentrically with the cutterhead. Is adjustable for height.

FLEXIBLE: A flexible spring steel pad or shoe is backed up by a rigid bar with toes which holds the work firmly and close to cutterhead. The bar swings concentrically with cutterhead and is adjustable for height.

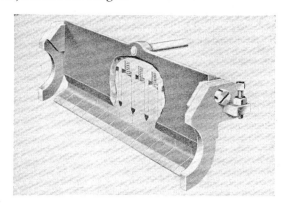

Cutaway view of sectional chipbreaker showing spring loaded individual sections and concentric end supports.

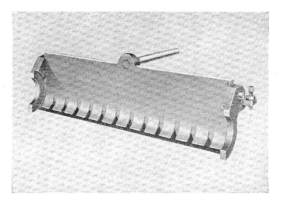

Flexible chipbreaker showing flexible steel pad, toes on bar and concentric end supports.

Fig. 4-31: Sectional & Flexible Chipbreakers. No. 29 & 32 Single Surface Planers. Baxter D. Whitney & Son Co. Circa 1935 Brochure.

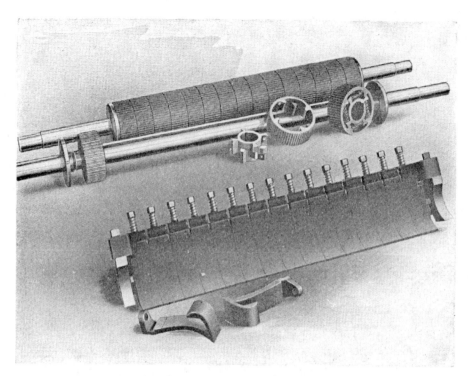

Sectional Feed Roll and Chipbreaker
Applicable to Nos. 444x6½ Surfacers

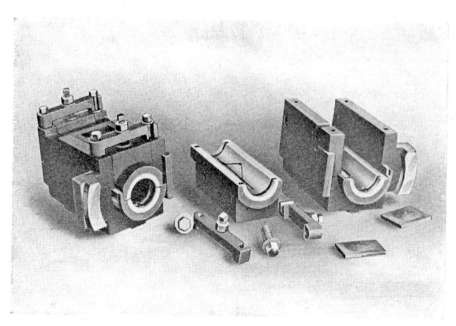

Detachable Side Clamping Boxes

Fig. 4-32: Sectional Infeed Roll & Chipbreaker. American Wood Working Machine Co.,
13th Ed. Catalog 1921.

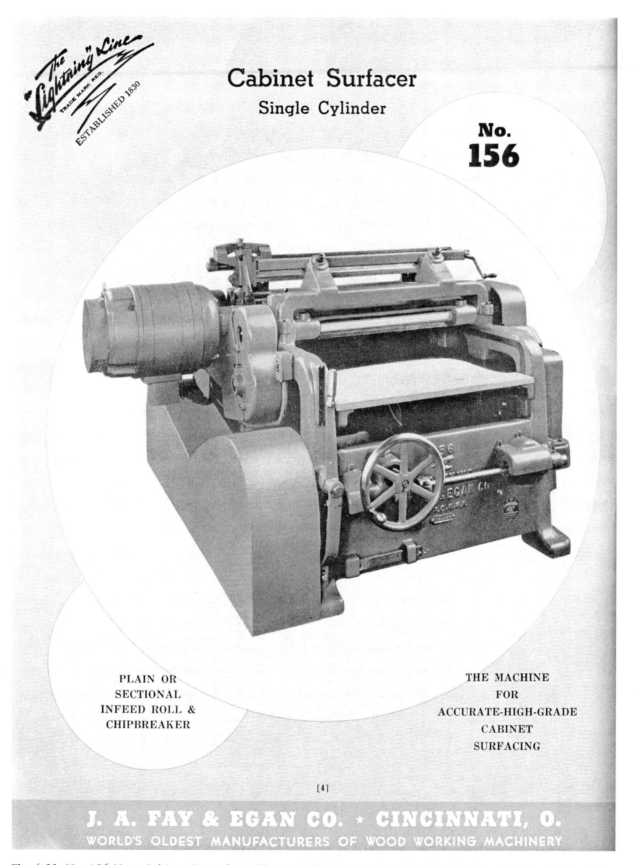

Cabinet Surfacer
Single Cylinder

No. 156

PLAIN OR
SECTIONAL
INFEED ROLL &
CHIPBREAKER

THE MACHINE
FOR
ACCURATE-HIGH-GRADE
CABINET
SURFACING

[4]

J. A. FAY & EGAN CO. ★ CINCINNATI, O.
WORLD'S OLDEST MANUFACTURERS OF WOOD WORKING MACHINERY

Fig. 4-33: No. 156 New Cabinet Smoothing Planer. With Spring Shoe On Chipbreaker. J. A. Fay & Egan Co.,
Sectional Catalog, 1910.

Right Front View of No. 110 Planer with Four-Speed Feed Motor.

Fig. 4-34: No. 110 Six-Roll Single Planer. With Four Speed Motor. Greenlee Bros. & Co., Circa 1944 Catalog.

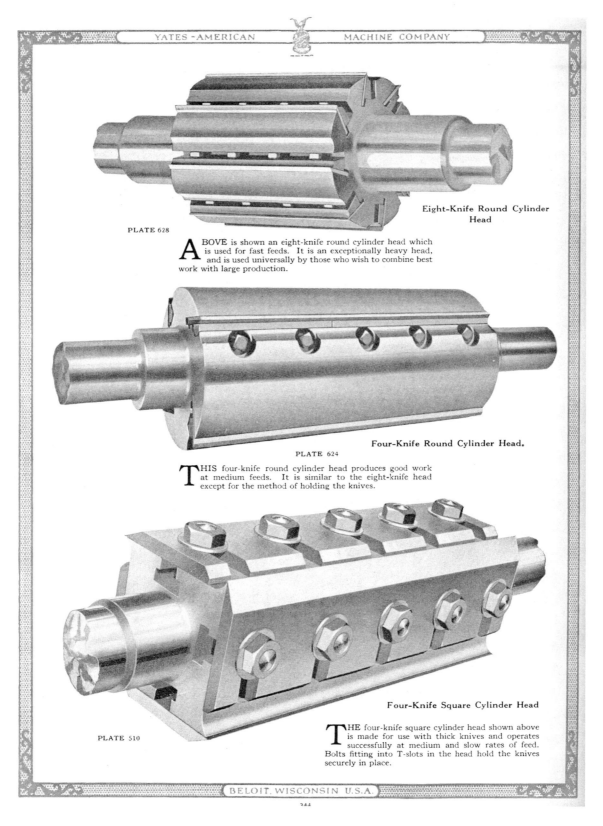

YATES-AMERICAN MACHINE COMPANY

Eight-Knife Round Cylinder Head

PLATE 628

ABOVE is shown an eight-knife round cylinder head which is used for fast feeds. It is an exceptionally heavy head, and is used universally by those who wish to combine best work with large production.

Four-Knife Round Cylinder Head.

PLATE 624

THIS four-knife round cylinder head produces good work at medium feeds. It is similar to the eight-knife head except for the method of holding the knives.

Four-Knife Square Cylinder Head

PLATE 510

THE four-knife square cylinder head shown above is made for use with thick knives and operates successfully at medium and slow rates of feed. Bolts fitting into T-slots in the head hold the knives securely in place.

BELOIT, WISCONSIN U.S.A.

Fig. 4-35: Square And Round Cutterheads. Yates-American Machine Co., Circa 1932 First Ed. Catalog.

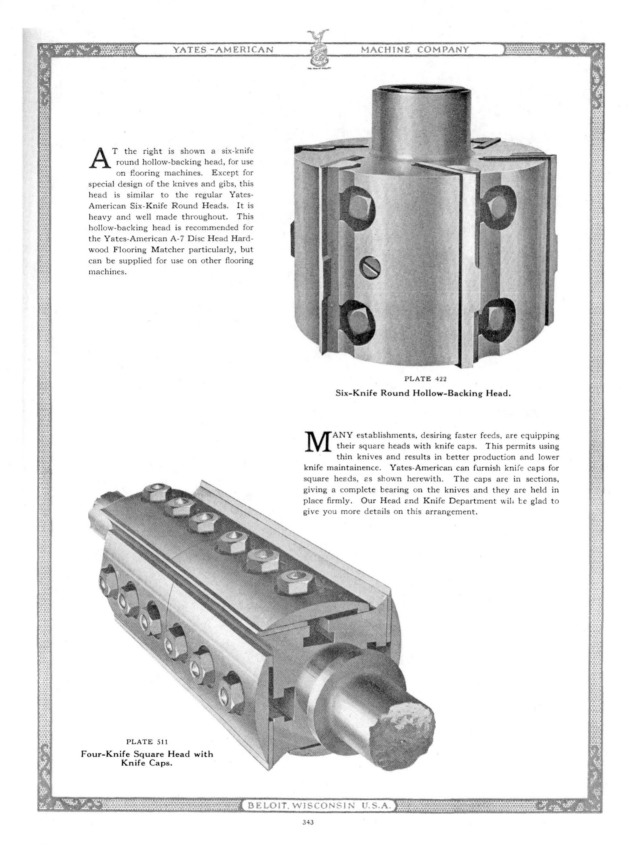

YATES-AMERICAN   MACHINE COMPANY

AT the right is shown a six-knife round hollow-backing head, for use on flooring machines. Except for special design of the knives and gibs, this head is similar to the regular Yates-American Six-Knife Round Heads. It is heavy and well made throughout. This hollow-backing head is recommended for the Yates-American A-7 Disc Head Hardwood Flooring Matcher particularly, but can be supplied for use on other flooring machines.

PLATE 422

Six-Knife Round Hollow-Backing Head.

MANY establishments, desiring faster feeds, are equipping their square heads with knife caps. This permits using thin knives and results in better production and lower knife maintainence. Yates-American can furnish knife caps for square heads, as shown herewith. The caps are in sections, giving a complete bearing on the knives and they are held in place firmly. Our Head and Knife Department will be glad to give you more details on this arrangement.

PLATE 511

Four-Knife Square Head with Knife Caps.

BELOIT, WISCONSIN U.S.A.

343

Fig. 4-36: Square Cutterhead. Yates-American Machine Co., Circa 1932 First Ed. Catalog.

Cylinder Head with Thin Knives—No. 511

WHERE thin knives mean better production and lower knife maintenance, knife caps as shown on this head can be furnished. These caps hold the knives securely in place and support them in the cut.

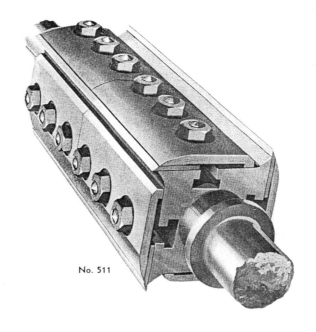

No. 511

Square Head for Pattern Work No. 441

DESIGNED for pattern work on shapers. Thick knives are furnished which clamp tightly to the head by means of square-headed bolts made of heat-treated alloy steel. Because of its great strength this head, when equipped with our heat-treated alloy steel bolts, can be operated at high spindle speeds with no danger of threads stripping or knives flying off.

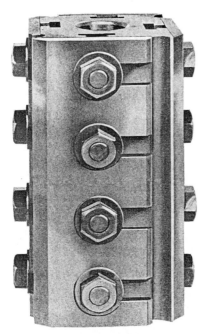

No. 441

Cylinder Head with Thick Knives—No. 510

TO operate at medium and slow rates of feed. Square-headed bolts as described above clamp the knives securely in place.

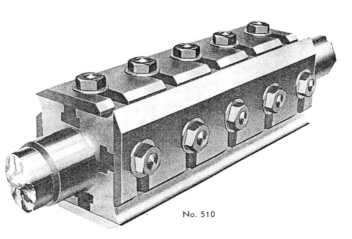

No. 510

Fig. 4-37: Various Square Heads. Yates-American Machine Co., Cutterhead And Knives Catalog, Circa 1950s.

Fig. 321

Motor Driven Planer

Motor Built on Planer Head

WITH this style of drive the flexible coupling is eliminated by mounting the high speed motor directly on the head of the planer. (Fig. 321). This makes a very convenient compact outfit where the No. 218, No. 224 and 26″ planer are to be driven by a motor attached direct to head.

Belted Motor Drive

THIS method of driving a planer with a motor requires a minimum of floor space and permits the use of any regular motor. (Fig. 204). The No. 218 and No. 224 and 26 by 8″ planers may be arranged in this way. In addition to the cost of planer and motor an extra charge is made for the motor mountings.

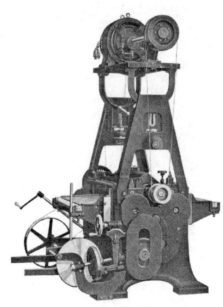

Fig. 204

Form 179-30M-9-25-24-24299   Printed in U. S. A.   J. J. Bennett, Printer, Lisbon, Ohio

Fig. 4-38: Motor Driven Planers. Crescent Machine Co., Aug. 25, 1924, Brochure.

104

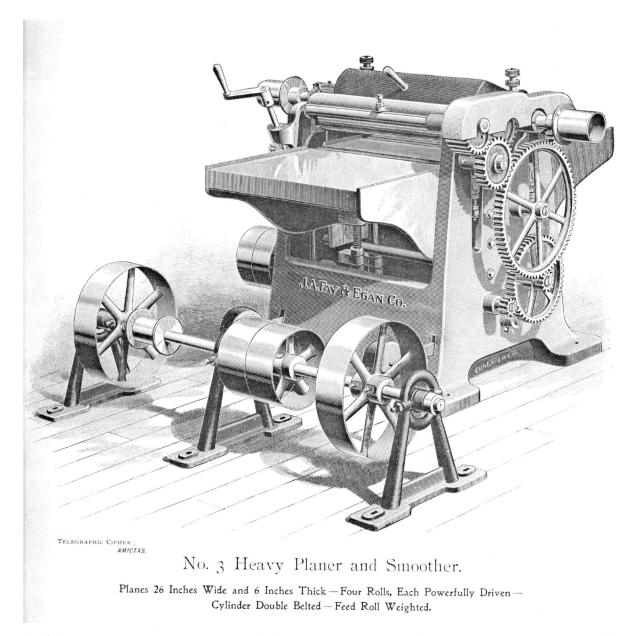

TELEGRAPHIC CIPHER:
AMICTAS.

No. 3 Heavy Planer and Smoother.

Planes 26 Inches Wide and 6 Inches Thick — Four Rolls, Each Powerfully Driven —
Cylinder Double Belted — Feed Roll Weighted.

Fig. 4-39: No. 3 Heavy Planer And Smoother With Countershaft. J.A. Fay & Egan Co., Catalogue Series L Circa 1901.

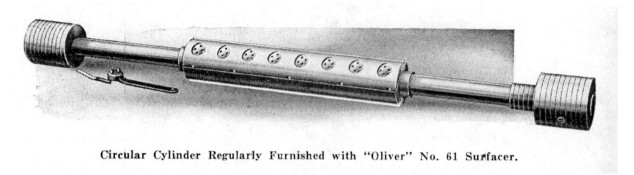

Circular Cylinder Regularly Furnished with "Oliver" No. 61 Surfacer.

Fig. 4-40: Round Cutterhead & Shaft With Slab Knife Holders. Oliver Machinery Co., Catalog No. 21, Circa 1920.

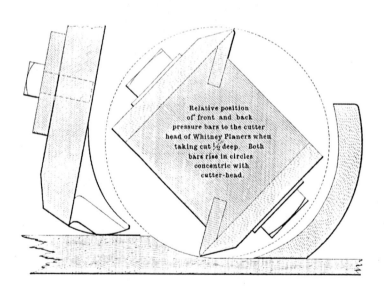

Relative position of front and back pressure bars to the cutter head of Whitney Planers when taking cut ⅛ deep. Both bars rise in circles concentric with cutter-head.

Fig. 4-41: Chipbreaker & Pressure Bar. Baxter D. Whitney & Son Co. 1898 Catalog.

30 x 6 Crescent Variable Feed Surfacer
(Patent applied for)

Fig. 4-42: 30 x 6 Variable Feed Planer. Crescent Machine Co. Catalog, 1912.

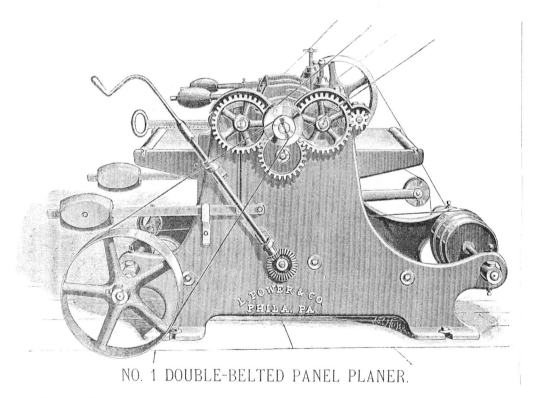

NO. 1 DOUBLE-BELTED PANEL PLANER.

Fig. 4-43: No. 1 Double-Belted Panel Planer. Idler Rolls Each End. L. Power & Co. Catalog, 1888.

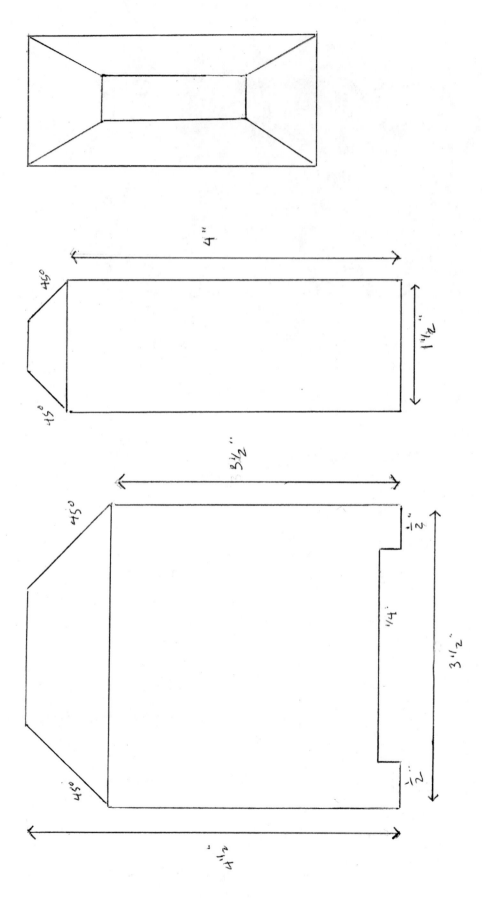

Fig. 4-44: Gage Block.

Chapter 5

TABLE ADJUSTMENT

Whether bolted to the floor or just held in place by sheer weight, a planer should be installed level and resting securely to prevent rocking or vibration. After snugging the machine to the floor a level is placed across the front or rear table. The table surface itself must be used as the reference point, not the table guides whether they are cast with the table or bolted on. The guides are not always the same height nor even machined. If you have to, raise the level above the guides by placing it on two wooden blocks of identical thickness. Level the machine by tapping hardwood shims beneath it. When tightening the bolts continue to watch the level and compensate with more shims if needed.

Next to the methods for holding the knives in the cutterhead, the mechanism for adjusting the table to be parallel to the cutterhead is the most variable. To do accurate planing, the table must be parallel with the cutterhead body. Lack of parallelism results in a taper over the width of the board.

Use a dial indicator or the gage block to check parallelism. Raise the bed until the gage just touches the cutterhead at one end. Raising the table into position keeps its entire weight on the adjusting screws or wedges; lowering the table into position can allow a slight looseness and cause inaccurate measurements. Do not check the table from the knives, since the knives could be out of alignment. The other end should just touch the gage block the same amount. If not, the table needs to be adjusted.

Another way to test is to feed two pieces of lumber simultaneously through the planer at the extreme right and left hand sides. Check the thickness of both pieces, they should be the same.

On planers such as the twin screw Powermatic No. 201, if the table is not parallel the gage is placed at the end that needs to be raised. The three socket head screws located beneath the table at that end are loosened. A rod is inserted into one of the open holes above and used to turn the shaft to raise the table until the gage contacts the cutterhead. The socket head screws are then re-tightened. The same effect can be achieved by lowering the other side of the table.

With the twin screw Powermatic No. 160 the gage is set under whichever side must be raised. The set screw that locks the threaded flange nut from rotation in the table is loosened on the side to be raised. The nut is rotated using a rod placed in the flange holes and that side of the table is raised until the indicator or the drag feel on the gage block is the same on both sides. The flange nut set screw is then re-tightened.

Another method is to loosen the set screw on the high side of the table and then rotate the table handwheel clockwise, raising the opposite side until it is level, and then re-tighten the flange nut set screw.

On Parks' standard 12" planer (Fig. 5-1), to raise the low side of the table the set screw on the bevel gear on the end of the table lifting screw at the opposite side of the planer is loosened. That side of the table will not be able to raise or lower when the handwheel is turned to bring the other side into alignment. Pressure must be maintained on the handwheel when the table is level until the loosened set screw is re-tightened.

On the Oliver No. 299 (Fig. 2-19) the table is adjusted for height by loosening three screws on the table, raising nuts under the table, turning the raising nut on the low side in the required direction and re-tightening the lock screw.

On Crescent's No. P-18 (Fig. 5-2) the set screw in the pinion on the cross shaft which raises the table on the high side is loosened and the pinion disengaged. The handwheel is then turned until the table is parallel with the cutterhead, after which the pinion is re-engaged and the set screw re-tightened.

On Delta's No. 22-101 the low side of the table is raised by first loosening the set screw in the adjusting nut on the lifting screw on that side. A 1/4" rod is inserted into the hole in the nut which is turned the required amount, and the set screw is re-tightened.

On Delta's No. 22-401 if an adjustment is necessary, the set screw under the end of the table that is to be adjusted is loosened and the adjusting nut turned the required amount; then the set screw is then re-tightened.

On wedge bed planers like Yates-American's J-180 (Delta's No. 22-212), to raise the table on the right side, the two square-headed screws located beneath the right side of the table (one on each side, running horizontally) are loosened. Then the two cap screws located below are loosened about two turns. The rear square head set screw is then loosened one or two turns. Then the front square head set screw is tightened one or two turns. This moves the upper wedge forward bringing the table into alignment. The cap screws are then re-tightened.

Beds raised and lowered by screws are guided by machined surfaces on the side panels. As the table raises and lowers, it bears against these machined surfaces, and over a period of time, they wear. To prevent the table from rocking and to compensate for this wear, two vertical gibs (metal bars) in front of the machine are held between the planer frame and the bed, one on each side. These gibs are adjusted individually using the screws provided so that they are lightly contacting each surface. If the table rises too freely or if it fits loosely in its track or ways, the gibs must be tightened.

Loosen the locknuts, usually three on each side, located on the front of the table and slightly tighten each set screw. If the table can be moved without undue effort, and if there is no perceptible play between the table and the ways, re-tighten the locknuts. The gibs should be tight enough to prevent rocking or movement of the table when the planer is in operation. If extra effort is required to move the table, the gibs may be too tight.

The finished planed thickness of the board is shown by a pointer and vertical scale. Usually the thickness gauge is located on the base. On rare occasions, such as on Frank H. Clement's 1898 No. 3 Improved Double Belted Surfacer (Fig. 5-3) and No. 1 Improved Planer And Smoother (Fig. 5-4), it takes the form of a metal bar and is mounted above.

The depth scale indicates the distance between the table and the bottom of the cutting circle. The best method for calibrating the readout is to simply put a board through the machine, measure its thickness, and set the scale to that measurement. The pointer with its slotted hole is usually secured by a screw. Loosen the screw, move the pointer up or down to the correct thickness, and re-tighten. The scale should be recalibrated after every knife change or if the knives are sharpened in the cutterhead. Adjusting the table parallel to the cutterhead may also require recalibrating.

12" x 4" BENCH TYPE THICKNESS PLANER

Model No. 95

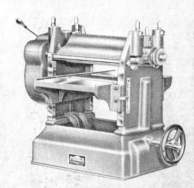

- CAST IRON CONSTRUCTION
- SMALL SHOP VERSATILITY
- BIG PLANER VERSATILITY

A real heavy duty machine that has been tested and approved in more than 50,000 shops all over the world. Incorporates the precision features of some of the finest and most expensive mill planers—and yet is priced within the budget of the smallest shop.

SPECIFICATIONS

CAPACITY-12" wide x 4" thick. Minimum thickness 1/16" and takes pieces as short as 6".

POWER-1 to 3 H.P. recommended.

FEED RATE-16 feet per minute. Positive action power feed rolls.

FRAME-Heavy, well-ribbed cast iron.

TABLE-One-piece, heavy ribbed cast iron, precision-planed for accuracy.

CUTTER HEAD-Heavy-duty, ball bearing safety-type head, 3 1/4-inch diameter, machined from solid bar steel. Precision built and accurately balanced. Has three knives of finest quality high-speed steel obtainable and micro-adjustment for quick, positive setting of knives.

BEARINGS-Heavy-duty ball bearings, equipped with Alemite fittings.

CHIP BREAKER-and pressure bar completely guard the head and feed rolls.

WEIGHT-244 pounds

12" x 4" DIRECT MOTOR DRIVE THICKNESS PLANER

Model No. 96

Machine specifications also the same as Model No. 95, shown at left above. Available without base for bench mounting. Available with 1 1/2 or 2 H.P. direct drive motor.

12" x 4" FLOOR MODEL BELT DRIVE THICKNESS PLANER

Model No. 97

Machine specifications are the same as for Model No. 95, shown above. The Model No. 97, however, is supplied complete with sturdy steel base (20" wide, 25 1/2" long, 22" high), motor, belts, pulleys, and heavy steel belt guard. Available with 1, 1 1/2, 2, or 3 H.P. motor.

12" PLANER — JOINTER COMBINATION

Model No. 11

- TWO MACHINES IN ONE
- SAVE YOU SPACE AND MONEY
- ONE MOTOR OPERATES BOTH

A sturdy combination machine that offers a considerable saving in machine investment for the shop that requires both a planer and jointer, since both machines are operated by one motor. Jointer unit is complete with knife and material guard.

12" PLANER SPECIFICATIONS

Same for Model No. 95, shown at left above.

12" JOINTER SPECIFICATIONS

CAPACITY-Will handle material up to 12" wide. Maximum cut is 3/16".

TABLES-Both tables are adjustable for depth of cut and are made of gray iron casting precision- planed for accuracy. Overall length of table is 33", width 12".

FENCE-Jointer unit comes complete with knife guard and tilting fence for bevel cutting. Fence tilts to 45°.

Fig. 5-1: 12" Planer. Parks Wood Working Machine Co.

CRESCENT
P-18 PLANER

18" x 6"

Fig. No. 544

Fig. 5-2: P-18 Planer. 15 to 45 fpm. Controlled By Reeves Variable Drive. Crescent Machine Co., Circa 1939 Brochure.

F. H. CLEMENT CO.'S

No. 3, Double Belted Surfacer, Improved.

Fig. 5-3: No. 3 Improved Double Belted Surfacer. Depth Scale Above Table. Frank H. Clement Co. American Wood Working Machine Co. First Edition Catalog, 1898.

No. 1, Planer and Smoother, Improved.

Fig. 5-4: No. 1 Improved Planer And Smoother. Available As 16, 20 & 24 x 6. Thickness Gauge Above Table. Forged Solid Steel Cutterhead. Frank H. Clement Co., American Wood Working Machine Co. First Edition Catalog, 1898.

Chapter 6

BED ROLL ADJUSTMENT

Adjusting the bed rolls is the simplest operation and a good learning experience since the mechanisms for supporting and adjusting the feed rolls, chipbreaker, and pressure bar are all very similar. The best method to set the bed rolls without a dial indicator is to first drop all the rolls below the bed's surface.

Typically each bearing of the roll, whether it is Babbitt, ball, or roller, is encased in a metal box also known as a roll or bearing box (Fig. 4-5) which is adjustable up or down within a snugly fitting frame that prevents the box from twisting. The simple mechanism for doing so is usually located directly beneath the box. It consists of a locknut and a bolt, set screw, or socket head screw (also called stud bolts or jack screws in various manuals) which bears directly against the box's bottom (Figs. 6-1 & 6-2). The screws supporting the roll guarantee it will drop no lower.

Unloosen the nut and unthread the bolt. The roll's end should move down just by its own weight. If not, give it a light tap with a dead blow mallet.

As a general rule, the rolls are set .003" above the bed when planing smooth lumber and at .015" for rough sawn lumber.

If the rolls are set too low, rough, heavy lumber can stall. This is often caused by a board with a kink or hollow valley on its underside. The board feeds until the hollow fails to make contact with a bed roll. When the board loses contact with the lower rolls, it becomes jammed between the pressure bar and table since the infeed and outfeed rolls may lack the power to overcome the increased friction and horse it through. Setting the rolls higher makes this less likely to occur.

Long bows in lumber will not cause the trouble short kinks do. The pressure of the feed rolls and the pressure bar flatten a long bow gradually as it passes through, but they have little or no effect on the short kinks which bridge the rolls.

After determining the required height for your planing conditions, place two pieces of the proper shim material or feeler gages on the bed, one just on the outside edge of the rear roll's slot, the other on the outside edge of the front roll's slot. Bridge both rolls with a level, its center above the bed's middle. Place a small weight on the level's center, just enough to hold it in position. A box of nails is ample. Raise each roll with the bolt or screw until it just touches the level. Re-tighten the locknut while holding the bolt securely. Otherwise the nut can change the setting. Repeat the procedure for the opposite ends.

Some perfectionists return to the other end and check the setting again on the theory that adjusting the opposite ends of the rolls may have changed their settings. In most cases, however, any difference is negligible.

On planers with two infeed bed rolls, some operators set the first bed roll slightly higher than the one closest to the cutterhead (Fig. 4-3). When this roll is slightly higher, the lumber is forced into a very slight, natural curve, which helps keep the lumber against the bed, directly under the cutterhead as it feeds through.

On Greenlee Brothers & Co.'s No. 110 Six-Roll Single Planer (Fig. 2-11) the bottom roll bearing cases are seated on wedges, with the adjustment within easy reach from the outside.

Only one wrench is necessary as the adjustments have spring locks.

It is important that both ends of the table rolls be the same height to help prevent skewing of the board as it feeds through.

The idler rolls located at the extreme ends of some planer beds (Fig. 4-43) should be set slightly higher than the other bed rolls. This gradual slope creates a slight, continuously lift on the ends and helps prevent snipe by keeping the board flat on the table.

If a planer refuses to feed after making the adjustments the trouble could be that some, or all, of the lower roll bearings are worn. Even when worn, the rolls can be adjusted perfectly, but pressure on the lumber causes them to sink in the bearings to a point where they cease to function properly, or not at all. This means the lower bearings must be replaced or re-Babbitted.

The bearings can be adjusted while under pressure by placing two pieces of lumber of equal thickness or width straight through the machine about 6" or 8" from each end of the rolls. The table is raised (with the power off) until the pieces exert pressure on the lower rolls while they are being set. This is a makeshift solution only.

Fig. 6-1: Bed Roll Adjustment On 24 x 8 John A. White Co. Planer, Circa 1876.

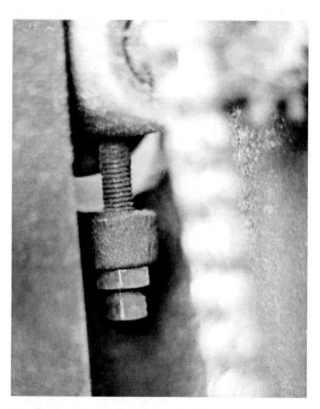

Fig. 6-2: Bed Roll Adjustment On 20 x 8 Buss Machine Works No. 208 Planer, Circa 1950.

Chapter 7

INFEED ROLL ADJUSTMENT

The infeed roll, like the bed rolls, has its bearing cases set in metal boxes that are guided in pockets machined in the side frames, so correct alignment is always maintained. Usually the adjusting bolts, set screws, or socket head screws and locknuts are either situated above each of the feed roll's extreme ends as with Powermatic's Model 201, or like the Buss No. 208 (Fig. 7-1) and Powermatic Model 100 are located beneath each end. The roll is raised or lowered by loosening the locknut and turning the set screw to the right to raise it, or to the left to lower. The roll on Oliver's No. 299 (Fig. 2-19) is adjusted for height by loosening the large locknuts on each end of the roll and adjusting a threaded bushing. Turning clockwise lowers the roll.

However, some planers have feed rolls that are not truly adjustable and bottom out, their distance preset in relation to the correct arc of the knives. This requires absolute accuracy in setting the knives.

On Yates-American's J-180 (Delta's No. 22-212) if the roll must be raised or lowered, both of the hexagon locknuts on the square headed screws, one above each roller end, are loosened and the lower locknut turned to the right to raise and to the left to lower. When equal settings are obtained, both locknuts are tightened against each other.

To adjust the infeed roll, use the gage block. Solid rolls should be set at 1/32" below the cutting arc of the knives, sectional rolls at 1/16". Place the block with its appropriate piece of shim material or a feeler gage on top of it under a knife in the cutterhead and raise the bed with its elevating handwheel until the knife just touches the feeler gage at its lowest point. Leaving the bed in the same position, remove the feeler gage and place the block beneath the extreme left and right ends of the roll. The block should touch the roll at its lowest point. If too high, lower the roll; if too low, raise the roll. Re-check both ends. Re-tighten the nuts when set. Don't over-tighten since the screws may need re-adjustment.

It is important that the setting on both sides of the roll be the same height to help avoid skewing of the material as it is fed through the machine.

Some manuals direct that after checking with a gage block that the cutterhead is parallel with the bed and setting the pressure bar, the remaining adjustments be done by lowering the bed in steps of 1/32", usually one half turn of the wheel. I've found it easier and more accurate to use the feeler gage method.

It's more practical to set the infeed roll, chipbreaker, pressure bar, and outfeed roll all at the same time since you have established a height from which all other parts can be adjusted. Just be sure to leave the bed in exactly the same position.

The top infeed and outfeed rolls, pressure bar, and chipbreaker are not made completely rigid. Each has some vertical movement, not only to allow for slight variations in thickness but also to prevent a dislodged knot or splinter caught up in the feeding system from damaging the machine. This is usually regulated by spring tension or weighted levers (Fig. 7-2).

The use of springs instead of weighted levers not only gives a more instantaneous and steady tension but also eliminates the pounding up and down strains common with weights.

The infeed roll is under constant tension and this tension must be just enough to feed the lumber steadily through the planer without slipping or hesitation but not so tight that it causes damage to the board.

Pressure should be adjusted by trial and error. Too much pressure on the roll will leave marks on the material if light cuts are being taken. Rough sawn and green material will require more pressure than smooth dry material. The tension should be equal at both ends of each roll to help avoid skewing of the material as it is fed through. Do not tighten the box springs so tight that the entire roll cannot move up if required to do so.

If possible, adjust spring tension by first unloosening the screws that compress the springs, then tighten. From the point where they first start to compress, tighten the springs about five to six turns depending on the spring. A trial run will tell whether more or less tension is required.

The tension on the infeed roll (and the outfeed) can be roughly judged by inserting a 4-foot 2 x 4 in the planer and lifting the roller and spring on one side and then the other and comparing the force required. With planers with weighted levers, simply lift up on one and then the other to test. Planers geared or belted on one side may require slightly more tension on the unsupported side to feed the lumber through without skewing.

On the Powermatic No. 100, the feed roll is held with a spring-loaded plunger slide with tension to regulate the pressure. Pressure on feed roller is regulated with a spring cap screw on each end. To increase pressure, turn the screw right, to decrease turn left.

On the Buss No. 208, pressure is varied by loosening the locknuts and adjusting the set screws above the roll boxes (Fig. 7-3). Spring pressure on the Oliver No. 299 (Fig. 2-19) is increased by tightening the two locknuts on the center stud.

On Delta's No. 22-101, the locknuts above roll on each end are loosened and the screws turned the required amount and the nuts re-tightened. Delta's No. 22-401 requires removing the side panels. The locknut is loosened and the spring retainer above each roll end is rotated to increase or decrease spring tension.

To increase the tension on machines equipped with weighted levers, loosen their bolts and slide the weights in for less pressure and out for more. Try to keep both at the same distance to prevent the wood from feeding through at an angle.

Fig. 7-2: Infeed Roll Spring Tension Adjustment On 20 x 8 Buss Machine Works No. 208 Planer, Circa 1950.

Fig. 7-1: Infeed Roll Adjustment On 20 x 8 Buss Machine Works No. 208 Planer, Circa 1950.

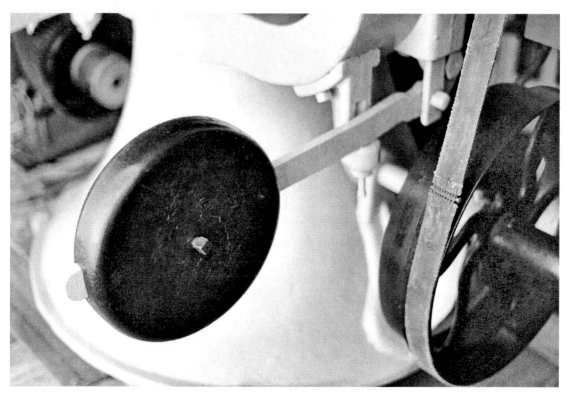

Fig. 7-3: Infeed Roll Pressure Adjustment On John A. White Co. Planer, Circa 1876. Pressure Increased By Moving Weights Outward On Levers.

Chapter 8

CHIPBREAKER ADJUSTMENT

When material is fed through, the chipbreaker should raise about 1/32" and it must always rest on the material while it is being planed. Therefore the chipbreaker in its free position should be 1/32" below the cutting arc of the knives. Too low a setting will cause undue pressure and retard the feed. Snipes on the front end of the lumber indicate the chipbreaker is set too high. Splintering or grain tear-out may also indicate the chipbreaker is set too high, or is not even contacting the material. It is also important that the setting on both sides of the chipbreaker be the same to help avoid skewing of the material as it is fed through.

The means of adjustment vary, though usually making use of a bolt, set screw, or socket head screw and a locknut. On the Buss No. 208 a set screw and locknut are located beneath each end of the sectional chipbreaker (Fig. 8-1). The locknut is loosened and the screw moved up or down. Another Buss model has a moveable arm that extends from the chipbreaker and rests on an adjustable screw and locknut supported on the planer's front housing.

On Powermatic's Nos. 201 and 160, a set screw or bolt and locknut are situated above each of the chipbreaker's extreme ends. The nut is loosened and the set screw moved in or out to adjust the height. The nut is re-tightened after setting. Because the chipbreaker-adjusting screws contact the bearing housings for the infeed roll, their adjustment should be made after adjusting the infeed roll. If the infeed roll setting is altered, the chipbreaker must be re-adjusted.

On many of the older planers, like the John A. White, the chipbreaker and shaving hood are joined, their combined weight serving to keep it down. The chipbreaker is self-adjusting, with a positive stop built in. This makes setting the knives correctly very critical. Some planers like Yates-American's J-180 (Delta No. 22-212) and Delta's Nos. 22-101 and 22-401 also require no adjustment and provide a uniform drag from left to right.

To adjust the chipbreaker, place the gage block with a 1/32" piece of shim stock or a feeler gage on top of it under a knife in the cutterhead and raise the bed until the knife just touches the feeler gage at its lowest point. Leaving the bed in the same position, remove the feeler gage and place the block beneath the extreme left and right ends of the chipbreaker. The block should touch the chipbreaker at its lowest point. If too high, lower the chipbreaker, if too low, raise the chipbreaker.

The chipbreaker rides the wood by its own weight or is combined with springs (Fig. 8-2) or weights. Adjust the spring tension by first loosening the screws to release the tension, then tighten. From the point where they first start to compress, tighten the springs about five to six turns depending on the spring. A trial run will tell whether more or less tension is required. On the Buss No. 208 a bolt is turned in or out to adjust the spring tension.

Fig. 8-1: Chipbreaker Adjustment On 20 x 8 Buss Machine Works No. 208 Planer, Circa 1950.

Fig. 8-2: Chipbreaker Spring Tension Adjustment On 20 x 8 Buss Machine Works No. 208 Planer, Circa 1950.

Chapter 9

PRESSURE BAR ADJUSTMENT

Improper setting of the pressure bar causes almost all planing problems. It is the most critical and most sensitive unit in the feeding system. The bar must be set at the same height (.000") as the knife at its lowest point. However, this initial setup is a starting point and final adjustment may have to be made after several test cuts. The bar may have to be set .001" higher or lower than the knife. When the knives are jointed, ground, or replaced, the pressure bar must be re-adjusted.

Like the bed rolls, the bar is fixed into a frame to keep it in line. Usually a bolt, set screw, or socket head screw and locknut is situated below each of the bar's extreme ends (Fig. 9-1). The height is regulated by loosening the locknut and moving the set screw in or out and re-tightening the nut when set. Various manufacturers, however, have designed different methods (Fig. 9-2). On the Buss No. 208 the locknut is loosened and the set screw turned in or out.

On Oliver Machinery Co.'s No. 299 (Fig. 2-19) the pressure bar is adjusted by loosening large locknuts on each end of the bar and adjusting a threaded bushing. Turning clockwise lowers the bar.

Yates-American Machine Co.'s J-180 (Delta's No. 22-212) wedge bed planer requires loosening all four locknuts (locknuts only, not square set screws) one in each corner located above the bar. To raise the pressure bar the rear set screws are loosened 1 or 2 turns and front set screws tightened 1 or 2 turns. To lower the pressure bar the procedure is reversed. After the pressure bar is adjusted, the locknuts are re-tightened.

On Delta's No. 22-101 the pressure is exerted by rubber pressure pads which can be adjusted if necessary.

The hexagonal nuts, washers, and pressure pads located on each end of the bar have to be removed first. Turning the adjusting nuts moves the pressure bar up or down. Turning the nut clockwise raises it; counterclockwise lowers it.

Afterwards, the pressure pads, washers, and hexagon nuts must be replaced. While holding the adjusting nut with a wrench, the hexagon nut compressing the rubber pressure pad is turned. Each nut must be turned the same amount.

On Delta's No. 22-401, if the pressure bar must be raised or lowered at either end, the socket head screw above the bar end is loosened and the adjusting screw turned the required amount, using a special wrench until the pressure bar just touches the gage block.

After the pressure bar is adjusted, the socket head screw is re-tightened with a wrench. To make sure the adjusting screw is not disturbed while doing so, it is held securely with the special wrench.

To determine the position of the pressure bar, use the gage block alone or with a .001" piece of shim stock or a feeler gage on top of it. Place it under a knife in the cutterhead and raise the bed with its elevating handwheel until the knife just touches at its lowest point. Leaving the bed in the same position, place the block beneath the extreme left and right ends of the bar. The block should touch the bar. If too high, lower the bar; if too low, raise the bar. Re-check both sides and also check the full length of the pressure bar. If the center is slightly low, adjust

122

both sides the same amount to bring the low point into line.

Too light a pressure on the bar can allow a board to force it up, especially on longer pieces. Too heavy of a pressure can cause lumber to bog down and even stall. Pressure on both ends should be the same to prevent lumber from feeding at an angle.

On some planers, like my John A. White, there are simple knobs which move the bar up or down. Springs pinched in between maintain a constant pressure (Fig. 9-2). The adjustment on the Buss No. 208 is typical (Fig. 9-3)—a bolt is turned in or out to adjust the spring tension.

Pressure on Crescent Machine Co.'s P-18 (Fig. 5-2) is done by first loosening a cap screw on top of the adjusting screws. Turning the adjusting screw right gives more pressure, left less pressure. After adjusting, the cap screws are re-tightened. But care must be taken to keep the adjusting screw from turning while tightening the cap screw. On the Oliver No. 299 (Fig. 2-19) spring tension is increased by tightening two locknuts on the center stud.

Run a board to test the setup and fine tune height and tension if required. If the bar is too high, a shallow clip will occur on each end of the board. If it is too low, the board will hit the edge of the bar and not feed through at all.

Fig. 9-1: Pressure Bar Adjustment On 24 x 8 John A. White Co. Planer, Circa 1876.

Fig. 9-2: Pressure Bar Adjustment On 20 x 8 Buss Machine Works No. 208 Planer, Circa 1950.

Fig. 9-3: Spring Tension Adjustment On 20 x 8 Buss Machine Works No. 208 Planer, Circa 1950.

Chapter 10

OUTFEED ROLL ADJUSTMENT

The means for adjusting the height of the outfeed roll are very similar to those of the infeed roll, usually a bolt, set screw, or socket head screw and locknut above or below the roll's bearing box (Fig. 10-1).

Planers like the Powermatic No. 201 have a set screw and locknut situated above each of the feed roll's extreme ends. The nut is loosened and the set screw moved in or out to adjust the height. The nut is re-tightened when set. On the Powermatic No. 100 and the Buss No. 208 the roll box is held up with stud bolts and is raised or lowered by loosening the locknut on the set screw and turning it to the right to raise, or to the left to lower. On Powermatic's No. 160 this is a set screw. On the Oliver No. 299 (Fig. 2-19) the roll is adjusted by loosening the large locknuts on each end of the roll and adjusting a threaded bushing. Turning clockwise lowers the roll.

The roll is set 1/32" below the arc of the cutterhead knives. It is important that the setting on both sides of the outfeed roll be the same height to help avoid skewing of the material as it is fed through the machine.

Place the gage block with a 1/32" piece of shim stock or a feeler gage on top of it under a knife in the cutterhead and raise the bed until the knife just touches the feeler gage at its lowest point. Leaving the bed in the same position, remove the feeler gage and place the block beneath the extreme left and right ends of the roll. The block should touch the roll. If too high, lower the roll; if too low, raise the roll.

The feed roll pressure should be adjusted by trial and error to determine the necessary tension for proper feeding. Adjust to where

material will feed steadily without hesitation or slippage of roll. It is important that the pressure be equal on both ends of the roll. On some machines which are geared or belted on one side only it may be necessary to make the pressure slightly higher on the opposite side to help avoid skewing of the fed material.

On the Powermatic 100, the roll is held by a spring-loaded plunger slide with tension to regulate the pressure. Pressure on the roll is regulated with spring cap screws. To increase pressure, the screw is turned right; to decrease, turned left. On the No. 160, pressure is controlled by springs and is adjusted by use of screws located on top of the side panels. On the Buss No. 208, the roll is spring loaded and the pressure can be varied by loosening the locknut and turning the bolt above the roll box (Fig. 10-1). On the Oliver No. 299 (Fig. 2-19) the pressure is increased by tightening the two locknuts on the center stud.

Fig. 10-1: Outfeed Roll Adjustment On 20 x 8 Buss Machine Works No. 208 Planer, Circa 1950.

Chapter 11

KNIFE ADJUSTMENT

While the means devised for holding the knives in a planer's cutterhead and the methods of setting them are varied, the same precautions and procedures should be followed. This applies both to round and square cutterheads.

Most often on modern planers the knife rests in a narrow slot milled in the cutterhead. It is held in placed by knife bars, also known as gibs, shims, and chipbreakers, with threaded holes. The bolts or screws in the bar are backed out, which wedges everything into place. To aid in adjusting the knives some manufacturers have the knives resting atop jack (lifting) screws or coiled springs which fit into drilled recesses in the head.

Installing the knives is an exacting process and not one to be rushed. The end-to-end and knife-to-knife relationship must be held to within .001" for accurate and smooth planing. To help avoid cutterhead distortion while installing a new set of knives, remove and replace one knife at a time in a gradual process.

Any adjustment to one knife should also be done to the remaining knives. Failure to do so may result in an out-of-balance cutterhead which can lead to bearing failure. When replacing knives make sure one end does not extend beyond the cutterhead. If one does it can strike the machine's frame with fatal results. Rotate the cutterhead by hand to double check.

Knives can be set using a commercial knife-setting device, most of which work off the cutterhead, or a dial indicator (Figs. 11-1 & 11-2). Some manufacturers provided a gage or jig specifically designed for quickly setting the knives on an individual machine. The oldest and cheapest method uses two identical hardwood strips roughly 1 x 4 x 24 inches. They are planed at the same time to guarantee identical dimensions. One stick, or the gage block, can also be used, simply by moving it from side to side.

Assuming that the table is parallel to the cutterhead, the bed rolls are dropped beneath the table. The knives are removed and all dust, pitch, and other accumulated foreign matter is cleaned from the slots, lifting screws, bolts, springs, and the gibs. Screws and bolts should be oiled before threading them in. Check the screws. If the threads appear worn or stripped or if their heads are becoming rounded, replace them.

The strips are stood up, one on either side under the cutterhead. The knives are placed into the cutterhead at approximately the right height, and the mechanism for holding them tightened just enough to barely hold them in place.

The tips of the knives should be approximately 1/8" beyond the cutterhead. The heel of the bevel should be 1/16" or less outside of the cutterhead and the top of the gib should be approximately 1/8" down from the tip of the knife (Fig. 11-3).

The bed is adjusted until one knife's edge just touches one of the strips when rotated by hand. Adjust the knife so both ends touch the strips. One end might require bumping up slightly with a hardwood block or moved down slightly by lightly tapping the back of the knife with a punch and hammer. Repeat the procedure until each knife just brushes the wood at each end. A fine dusting of chalk on top of the strips helps to judge the setting. If the knife comes up with fine wood particles, the knife is too low; if it has a bit of chalk on it, it is set correctly. If there is nothing, it is too high. This method works particularly well with square-headed planers. Check both ends and the center. If a knife is bowed slightly in the center, raise or lower both ends to bring the center up to the gage, and then tighten the center knife screws.

On all planers, if all the knives have been removed, a new set must be installed gradually with all the gib screws lightly snugged down but not fully tightened. All the knives and gibs should be in place before final adjustment and tightening. If one knife is locked tightly before the others are tightened, the cutterhead may be sprung and cause uneven knife height and vibration.

The tightening process should always proceed working from the center out on each knife. After locking all the gibs screws once, again rotate the cutterhead by hand, and repeat the same sequence until all the screws are equally tight.

After installing the knives, re-check all the gib screws. Loose gib screws can result in knives being thrown out of the cutterhead, causing severe damage to the machine and possible serious or fatal injury to the operator or bystanders.

Triangular shear knife cutterheads like Bentel & Margedant Co.'s (Figs. 2-20, 2-35, 2-36, 2-48) are treated the same way. The knives themselves have straight edges and are set and ground the same as knives on other planers.

On the Powermatic No. 201, six hex-head screws hold in each knife. After threading them into the gib, the spring-loaded knife rises up in the slot. The knife is carefully removed from the cutterhead by lifting it straight out. The springs and the gib are put back into place and a new or re-sharpened knife is slipped in and the hex head screws are loosely snugged up.

The No. 201's Y-shaped knife-setting gage (sometimes called a crow's foot) is carefully placed on one end of the cutterhead spanning the knife slot. Its base depresses the springs and holds the tip of the knives to the proper height above the cutterhead (approximately 1/8"). If correct, that end is snugged up a bit more to hold the knife in place. The gage is used at both ends of the knife and then used to check the center

section to be sure it is even. If it is low, backing off slightly on the center gib screw will allow the blade to come up. If high, it is gently tapped down with a piece of hardwood until it conforms to the gage height. The full length of the knife is re-checked. Then the hex head screws are backed out until all are equally tight.

Delta's No. 22-101 follows the same system but has its own special bridge type setting gage. While the gage presses down and holds the knives in place the gib screws are gradually tightened.

Powermatic's Nos. 160 and 225 use a lifter or jack screw (a small, center threaded steel cylinder or plug with a hollow socket head) to adjust the knives. With the slots emptied and cleaned, the lifters are dropped back into place, the notched surface facing the knife slot, and the set screws threaded in until they bottom out.

With the knife and gib against each other and the beveled surface of the knife on the lifter side and the concave shaped surface of the gib up, everything is inserted into the slot. The bottom of the knife rests on the notch or step in the lifter. The set screw is screwed in until the knife just starts to rise on the lifter. The two outside and center gib screws are lightly tightened just enough to hold knives firmly in the head.

The knife tip is raised or lowered until it projects approximately 1/8" from the cutterhead body. The crow's foot is placed on the cutterhead and moved back and forth over the knife edge while using the wrench to raise or lower the knife. When the knife edge just ticks the crow's foot base, the right height has been reached. Both right and left are checked. Finally, the center section is checked to be sure it is within tolerance. If it is too low, backing off slightly on the center gib screw should correct it. The heel of the bevel should be 1/16" or less outside of the cutterhead body and the top of the gib should be approximately 1/8" down from the tip of the knife. Set the other knives the same way. If everything is correct, re-tighten.

There is a mistaken idea that knife lifters also serve the purpose of holding the knives in the cutterhead, and that the tighter they are secured in the cutterhead, the more secure are the knives. Not so. The lifters are only for positioning the knives. After the knives are set and locked in place, the lifters should be tightened only with firm pressure. If the lifters are being frequently sheared, this indicates either too much pressure is being put on them, or the knife gibs have not been tightly secured in the cutterhead.

This method seems to be the most popular. A similar setup is used on Parks machines, Yates-American's No. J-180 (Delta No. 22-212), Delta No. 22-401 and Buss planers. On some planers, like my Buss, the gibs and their slots in the cutterhead are numbered and should always correspond (Figs. 11-4 & 11-5).

The Crescent Machine Co. had a more sophisticated method based on the lifter method (Figs. 11-6 & 11-7).

The knife was held in place by a heavy steel throat-piece clamped firmly into position by key-plugs placed at intervals in sockets drilled into the body of the cutterhead and numbered. Each of these key-plugs was cylindrical in shape, with a flat place milled off on its side, making it wedge-shaped. A hollow set screw passed through the center of the key-plug, bearing against the bottom of the socket, and thrust the key-plug outward on its taper, causing it to key tightly and evenly against the throat-piece, thus holding the knife very firmly over its entire width. A very slight tightening of the screws, with the combined wedging action of the key-plugs, was sufficient to hold the knife firmly.

There was no tensile strain on the screws, as was the case with other forms of construction. With this the danger of accidents caused by broken screws was entirely eliminated. The small end of each key-plug was placed outward, so that it could not fly out even if the screw were loosened, but would tend to tighten from its own centrifugal force. Neither could a gib fly out, as it had a tongue along its lower edge fitting into a groove milled in the head. The knife was firmly supported by the solid metal of the head on its entire back surface, close to the cutting line. The space in front of the knife was completely filled by the gib, so there was no possible chance for chips to drive under the

knife, thus eliminating another common source of danger.

The knives were removed by first loosening the hollow set screws that past through the center of the key-plugs, by giving a half-turn to the left with a special hexagon wrench supplied with the machine. Before taking the wrench out, a blow was struck on top of the wrench with a light hammer to release the key-plug from its wedged position in the cutterhead. Since the key-plugs were wedge-shaped with their thick end toward the center of head, they had to be driven downward toward the center of cutterhead to loosen, after the screw was released. When all the key-plugs were released, the knife was free and could readily be removed. After the knife was removed, the gibs and key-plugs could also be removed.

To replace a knife, each key-plug was placed in its proper place according to the stamped numbers. After the key-plugs, gib, and knife were properly placed, the key-plugs were tightened very lightly, just enough to hold them in place. A special key wrench was then inserted into a hole, back from the knife. A lip on the end of the wrench projected under the lower edge of the knife, and by turning the wrench slightly, the knife was brought forward accurately, as far as required. A small gauge was supplied to indicate when the knife was in the correct position. When the knives were set, they were firmly clamped by tightening up the key-plugs.

Setting the knives on a square cutterhead is not much different than setting those on a round (Fig. 11-8). The knives are fastened directly to the cutterhead by bolts and washers, which either thread directly into the head or are fastened from behind by nuts in a Tee-slot milled in the cutterhead. If possible, the bolts, washers, nuts, and knives should always be returned to their original locations since they have been worn into position.

After cleaning the cutterhead's surfaces, the knives, and all the fasteners, thread the bolts about 1/2" into the head, they will help support the knife while you work. Move a knife roughly into position. The knife tip should project about 1/8" past the flat chipbreaker edge or lip of the cutterhead. Snug up the bolts in the slots just enough to hold it in place. Use your gauging system to fine tune the position and then tighten the bolts firmly. You're more apt to cut yourself on these fully exposed knives so use a hardwood block to tap them up or down accordingly.

Fig. 11-1: Knife Setting Gauge. P. B. Yates Machine Co. Catalog No. 14, Circa 1917.

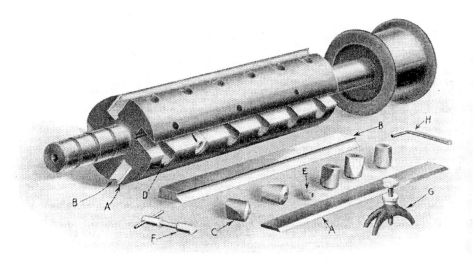

Fig. 11-2: Setting Knives. Crescent Machine Co., 1921 Catalog.

Crescent Planers

(Patented)

General Description

CRESCENT Planers and Planers and Matchers are exceptionally well constructed of best materials throughout and may be depended upon to turn out large quantities of satisfactory work at a low cost for upkeep.   The machines are neat in design, well proportioned throughout and the following general features of construction are embodied in all sizes.

The Frame is cored out hollow cast in one piece, heavily ribbed to make it strong, rigid and free from vibration.   The design, together with the weight of the frame insures proper alignment of the working parts at all times.

The Bed is gibbed direct to the outside of the frame.   This construction makes it easy to adjust, prevents bed from rocking and avoids clipping the ends of lumber.   An idler roller is placed at each end of the bed to facilitate the feeding of lumber. The top of bed is planed perfectly true and has ledges at sides to hold the lumber within the limits of the knives.

The Chip-Breaker and Pressure Bar are placed as close to the knives as easy clearance will allow and make it possible to plane very short stock.   When taking a heavy cut, the raising of the front roll will partially raise the chip breaker so as to admit the lumber.   The 18 and 24 inch planers and planers and matchers are equipped with solid chip breakers, but when specially ordered, the 26 inch planer may be supplied with a sectional chip breaker at an additional price.

The Rolls are milled from a solid bar of steel, finished and machined all over, the upper in-feeding roll is corrugated, and the other rolls have face ground true and smooth.   On the 18 and 24 inch planers and on the Crescent planers and matchers the upper rolls are driven, but on the 26 inch machine all four feed rolls are driven by gears. Solid in-feeding roll is furnished on the 18 and 24 inch planer and on the Crescent planers and matchers, but on the 26 inch machine we can supply a splendid sectional feed roll at a slight additional price.

The Heads are milled from a solid bar of steel, of proper grade of carbon, carefully balanced and with bearings ground absolutely true and smooth. The 18 inch and 24 inch planers and Crescent Planers and Matchers have rectangular heads fitted with two knives and the 26 inch planer has

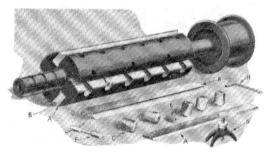

Fig. 136

two knife square head.   The Crescent Patented Round Safety Head (Fig. 136) fitted with four knives may be supplied at a slight additional price.

The Bearings for the Head are cast solid with the frame and are entirely free from complication. They are lined with best grade of high speed babbitt and are provided with liners to adjust for wear. Bearings are provided with an oil chamber filled with capillary felt to make them practically self-oiling and self-closing oil hole covers exclude all dust and dirt.   All other bearings of the machine are provided with self-closing oil hole covers where possible.

Fig. 11-3: Safety Head. Crescent Machine Co., Aug. 25, 1924, Brochure.

Machine Knives

Machine Knives. The knives regularly used in Crescent Round Safety Heads are made of high speed steel, specially treated to give continued satisfactory service, rigidly guaranteed, require a minimum of sharpening and are very economical to use.

Safety Heads for Jointers

Fig. No. 136. **Round Safety Heads** are regular equipment on all Crescent Jointers and Planers but may be made specially to order to fit machines of other makes.

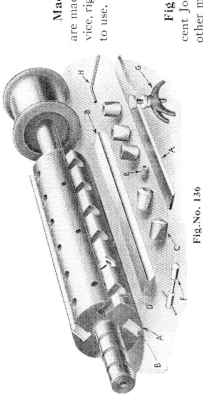

Fig.No. 136

Fig. 11-4: Round Cutterheads Standard On Jointers & Planers. Crescent Machine Co., 1930 Catalog.

4 THE CRESCENT MACHINE COMPANY

Directions for Taking Knives Out of Safety Head

FIRST loosen the hollow set screws that pass through the center of the key-plugs, by giving about a half-turn to the left with the hexagon wrench sent along for that purpose. Before taking wrench out, strike a blow on top end of wrench with a light hammer to release the key-plug from its wedged position in the head. The key-plugs are wedge shape with their thick end toward center of head, therefore have to be driven a blow downward toward center of head to loosen, after screw is released. When all the key-plugs are thus released, then the knife will be free and can readily be removed. After knife is removed, the throat-piece and key-plugs can also be removed.

To replace the knife, first see that all the dirt and dust is removed from the knife seat and throat-piece. See that each key-plug is in its proper place according to the numbers stamped on the same.

After the key-plugs, throat piece and knife are properly placed, tighten the key-plugs, very lightly; then insert the knife adjusting wrench "F" into hole back of knife. A lip on the end of wrench projects under the lower edge of knife. By turning the wrench slightly the knife is brought up accurately as far as desired. The knife setting gauge "G" indicates when knife is in proper position. When knives are properly set, they should be clamped firmly in position by tightening the hollow set screw with the wrench "H" shown on page 2. This arrangement makes it easier to set the knives on a Crescent round safety head than on the old style square head.

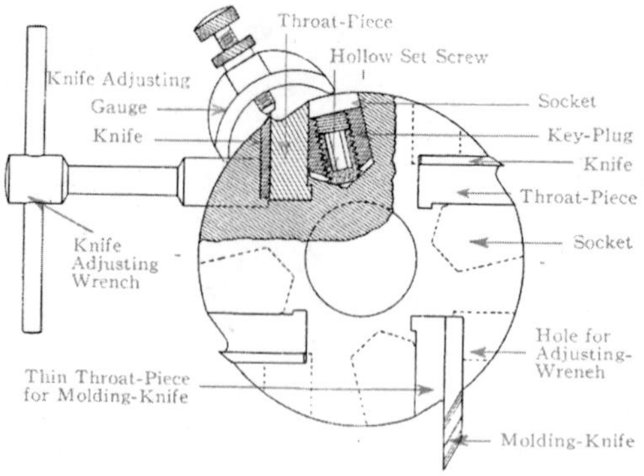

Fig. 148

The Crescent Safety Shaper Head

(Patented)

THE CRESCENT SAFETY SHAPER HEAD is a natural development form experience gained in the manufacture of Crescent Round Safety Heads for Jointers and Planers. The heads are made on the same principle as the Crescent Safety Jointer Heads with the exception that they are bored out for use on a shaper spindle. When used with straight knives they have all the advantages of a Safety Jointer Head.

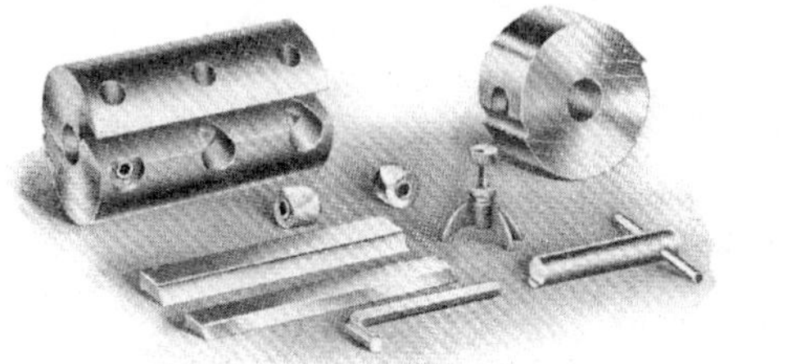

Fig. 209

The Crescent Safety Shaper Heads are regularly made with $4\frac{1}{4}$ inch diameter cutting circle and have two knives $\frac{1}{4}$ inch thick, $1\frac{3}{16}$ inch wide. Diameter of mandrel hole for Crescent Shapers 1 inch.

	Length of Head	Code Word
Head No. 4	2 inches	Dacen
Head No. 8	4 inches	Daisy
Head No. 12	6 inches	Daros

Each head is furnished with a pair of straight knives, knife-adjusting wrench, key-plug wrench, and knife gauge.

Special Sizes of heads will be made to order; and the following schedule shows the largest mandrel hole, and the number of knives that can be put in a head, for the various diameters of cutting circle.

Cutting Circle	Maximum Hole	Number of Knives	Cutting Circle	Maximum Hole	Number of Knives
$3\frac{3}{8}$	1	2	$4\frac{1}{8}$	$1\frac{11}{16}$	2 or 4
$3\frac{1}{2}$	$1\frac{1}{8}$	2	$4\frac{1}{4}$	1	2 or 4
$3\frac{5}{8}$	$1\frac{1}{4}$	2	$4\frac{3}{8}$	$1\frac{1}{8}$	2 or 4
$3\frac{3}{4}$	$1\frac{3}{8}$	2 or 4	$4\frac{1}{2}$	$1\frac{3}{16}$	2 or 4
$3\frac{7}{8}$	$1\frac{7}{16}$	2 or 4	$4\frac{5}{8}$	$1\frac{5}{16}$	2 or 4
4	$1\frac{5}{8}$	2 or 4	$4\frac{3}{4}$	$1\frac{1}{2}$	2 or 4

The smallest diameter of head that will be made is $3\frac{3}{8}$ inches; and the shortest head that will be made is 2 inches.

Crescent Safety Tenoner Heads have become quite popular. Being accurately machined and carefully balanced they insure a steady running tenoner that will show an increased production of accurate work. Tenoner heads are carried in stock only for Crescent tenoners. They are $6\frac{1}{2}$ inches diameter, $1\frac{1}{8}$ inch bore, $3\frac{1}{4}$ inches face. Special sizes may be made to order when proper measurements are given.

Guaranty. All Crescent Safety Heads are guaranteed to be free from all defects of workmanship or material and any head that fails from such cause will be replaced or repaired without charge.

Form No. 188—15M—1-30-25—24646JJB Printed in U. S. A. J. J. Bennett, Printer, Lisbon, Ohio

Fig. 11-5: Directions For Taking Out Knives. Crescent Machine Co., Jan. 30, 1925, Brochure.

Fig. 11-6: Slotted Knives. 24 x 8 John A. White Co. Planer, Circa 1876.

Fig. 11-7: Round Cutterhead And Knife On 20 x 8 Buss Machine Works No. 208 Planer.

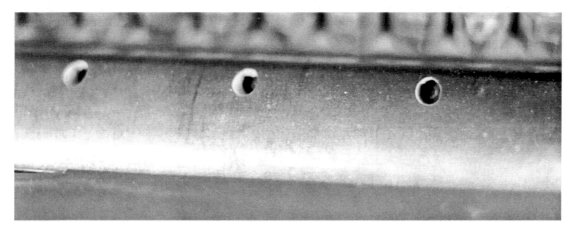

Fig. 11-8: Round Cutterhead And Knife On 20 x 8 Buss Machine Works No. 208 Planer.

Chapter 12

TROUBLESHOOTING

To test your initial setup use a piece of semi-finished lumber about three feet long and at least 3/4" thick. Set the depth of cut for 1/16". Start the planer, and standing to the left or right side, begin feeding the lumber into the machine.

The infeed roll should engage the material and push it under the chipbreaker and cutterhead. If the material feeds through effortlessly, examine the finished cut carefully. Learning to read a board for imperfections can save hours wasted in making needless adjustments.

If the board hangs up, turn the machine off, disconnect the power, lower the bed, remove the board, and then make adjustments. Never adjust anything while the machine is running. Make another test cut. The material should feed through smoothly.

HALTED FEEDING

If the wood isn't grabbed by the infeed roller, the table may be too low or the infeed roll too high. Remember that rough lumber requires that the table rolls be set higher.

If the infeed roll takes lumber away from you while feeding, then feeding stops immediately, the chipbreaker is probably too low, causing material to hit high on the heel. Reset the chipbreaker. Other causes could be that the chipbreaker pressure is too high, the feed roll is fractionally too high or the bed roll fractionally too low. Too great a pressure on the infeed roll can also cause stalling.

. If the infeed roll takes the lumber, the chipbreaker lifts, and just as you hear the knives contact the material, it stops feeding, the pressure bar is set wrongly.

About 90% of the time, the pressure bar is too low and the board is catching its leading edge. Remember that as the sharp edge of the planer knives wear, you must compensate for this wear by raising the pressure bar an equal amount on each side. Your first indication of knife wear is hesitation in feed of the material through the machine after it leaves the infeed roll on its way out of the machine.

If the wood sticks just after leaving the grip of the infeed roll, the tension on the outfeed roll may need to be increased slightly. The outfeed roll may even leave a faint rub mark where it's slipping. Make sure the tension is the same on both ends of the outfeed roll.

Poor feed can also be caused by oil or grease on the feed rolls, a rough or dirty bed, or belt slippage. Be sure the table is clean. Dusting the surface with talc or a coat of rubbed out paste wax occasionally will aid in smoother feeding and help prevent pitch buildup. Belt slippage can be corrected by increasing their tension or applying belt dressing. In very rare cases the trouble can be traced to feed rolls that are actually too smooth. Lightly roughening the feed roll with fine sandpaper will solve the problem.

STALLED LUMBER

Occasionally a board has thin spots caused by a wandering saw at the mill or some other malfunction. Sometimes such a board will only feed to the point where the thin spot comes up under the top infeed roll and then stalls. This is because the board is no longer thick enough to be gripped by it.

136

Vintage planers were equipped with weights to maintain a greater downward pressure on the lumber than could be achieved by the weight of the roll itself. Some of these had foot or hand levers and by bearing down on them enough additional downward pressure could be exerted momentarily to start such a board again and get it past the thin spot.

With weighted, sectional roll machines, additional boards should not be feed into the machines when this happens. Simply wait until the thicker pieces have all past under the infeed roll. The weights will react to bring the roll firmly down on the stalled board and it will then feed through with no problem.

Remember, the rolls are always trying to move the lumber along so any kind of movement given to the lumber manually may start it again. Try see-sawing the board from side to side. Sometimes a small pull sideways will start the board again. A push or a pull will also help.

If nothing works, stop the machine, remove the board, and either joint it or discard it.

CRUSHED CORNERS

This condition occurs with a sectional infeed roll when soft, narrow material is being run into the machine in such a way that the entire spring action of a segment bears down along one edge. To avoid it, feed the material so two segments bisect it, distributing the force more equally.

WASHBOARD FINISH

Don't confuse this with the shallow cut marks made by the knives. This is a very pronounced condition down the full length of the board. It results from one knife being too high and forced to do all the cutting. Reset the knives accordingly. (Fig. 12-1)

CLIP MARKS

If clip marks occur at equal distances from each end of the board, the pressure bar is too high. The marks look like half circles. Lower the pressure bar slightly on both ends and continue

to make test cuts and re-adjust the bar accordingly until they disappear. Sometimes the spring tension must be increased. (Fig. 12-2)

SNIPES

If snipes (long dished-out circular grooves) appear on one end of the board, a bed roll is too high causing a slight lift of the board as it passes through the machine. Try lowering the rolls by .001". Loose table gibs can also cause this effect.

Usually snipes are more noticeable on the trailing end of the board than on the lead end, and most often occur during planing of rough lumber. The rear bed roll may be too high causing the board to "teeter" and be planed deeper.

All the bed rolls must be elevated for running rough or resawn lumber through the machine. Keep in mind that when planed material is turned over to surface the other side, if you neglect to lower the bed rolls for a finished cut, snipes will appear on the ends of the board.

Also check the pressure bar. If it is too high, it will allow the board's end to lift up after it leaves the pressure of the infeed roller.

Snipes can also result from uneven feed roll pressure front to back; dull knives; or long, unsupported boards which are levering up the pressure bar and "bouncing" against the knives.

Snipe can be minimized but not eliminated. (Fig. 12-3)

CHATTER

Resembling the washboard finish, but on a finer scale, these marks usually appear on very thin material of 1/8" or less.

This is caused by the frail material actually bending down or bowing under each knife cut because the bed rolls are set too high. It does not happen to thick lumber because its stiffness resists the bowing effect.

A lack of stiffness can also cause the thin lumber to tear out badly. The infeed rolls push the lumber under the chipbreaker into the cutterhead and under the pressure bar. At this point the pressure bar begins to create friction. This first end is put under endwise compression by the infeed rolls still pushing behind it. This causes the thin material to buckle. It can't buckle down because of the bed so it buckles upward. When it buckles upward it will chatter under the continual downward thrust of the rotating cutterhead. If the buckling is severe, pieces of full thickness will be torn out.

Even at their lowest point, the bed rolls are too high to handle ultra thin material. Solve the problem by either using a slave board (a thicker piece of lumber wide enough and long enough to support the thin material with a cleat at the rear to keep the thin material from being pushed off) or make an auxiliary table out of countertop material that bridges the rolls, with cleats at each end to keep it stationary. (Fig. 12-4)

LONGITUDINAL RIDGES

A small raised ridge(s) running parallel to the board indicates the knives have been nicked. Shift two of the knives. One no more than 1/4" to the left, the other no more than 1/4" to the right. Make sure the shifted knives will clear the frame before starting the machine. (Fig. 12-5)

CHIP MARKS

These embossed marks are caused by shavings occasionally being tossed onto the finished surface of the board after leaving the cutterhead. They are consequently pushed down flush with the board's surface by the pressure of the upper outfeed roll. When removed they leave shallow indentations.

Most planers are designed with a shroud or cover over the top outfeed roll to help keep shavings from falling onto it. The author's Buss No. 208 lacks such a cover since an exhaust hood was recommended.

Usually the dents can be removed by slightly dampening the area and lightly sanding the dried raised grain. An exhaust system is recommended where efficient operation is a must. It can be eliminated if the planer sees occasional use and where the machine rollers have been designed with shrouds or wipers to keep them free of shavings. A malfunction in the exhaust system or too fast a feed can also cause the condition.

Accumulated pitch and dirt on the outfeed rolls can also mar the lumber. The upper outfeed roll should be checked more carefully than the lower, since it is in constant contact with the freshly machined surface.

TAPER

If the machine planes a taper across the full width of the board, the table is not parallel with the cutterhead. First check that all the knives are properly installed with equal protrusion from the cutterhead. If they are, then the table itself must be adjusted. But the table itself can account for the trouble.

On the older machines it is not uncommon to actually see that the bed's middle section has been worn down. I've seen them as much as 1/8" out. All inexperienced operators instinctively run boards down the planer's center instead of staggering the lumber across the surface.

Besides a taper, other signs of a worn table are: lumber run at the sides comes through in better condition than those that run through the center, or wide boards that are smooth on the outward edge but rough at another. This indicates the lumber is now being properly supported only at certain points. The pressure bar (perhaps worn itself), even when adjusted properly, is now too loose across the center to hold the lumber down with any firmness and is allowing it to vibrate.

The only real way to correct the situation is to remove the bed and have it ground flat again, an expensive proposition. However, you can work around this problem by simply continuing to run material down the middle and taking light cuts. The light pressure will allow the board to bridge the gap instead of being forced down into it. (Fig. 12-6)

TWISTING

If material twists (angles right or left) while feeding through the planer, the bed rolls, pressure bar, or feed rolls may be out of level. Re-check and re-adjust where required.

Generally the pressure bar will be out of level due to its constant adjustment to compensate for knife wear.

CHAIN JUMPING

This can be caused by inadequate tension, misaligned sprockets, or worn sprockets.

FUZZY, ROUGH, OR RAISED GRAIN

This can be caused by too heavy a cut, high moisture content, or dull knives. Lumber with a moisture content of 5–8% produces the best planed surface. Chipped grain, raised grain, and fuzzy grain increase in proportion with higher moisture content. If lumber has been kiln-dried too quickly, the holding power between the wood's hard and soft grain is lessened, and raised grain may occur. Rarely, but sometimes this is due to a severely worn table.

TORN GRAIN

This may be due to too heavy a cut, dull knives, or planing against the grain. Tear-out on cross-grained lumber can be minimized by feeding the lumber through the planer at an angle. Much like making a skew cut on a jointer. However, you must make sure that the angled board can pass through the planer without striking the planer's table guides or frame.

ROUNDED OR GLOSSY SURFACE

Dull knives are "polishing," not cutting the wood. The dull knives, instead of planing, pound the hard summer wood down, driving it into the soft spring wood. After the pressure of the knives is released, the summer wood gradually raises above the pressed-down spring wood.

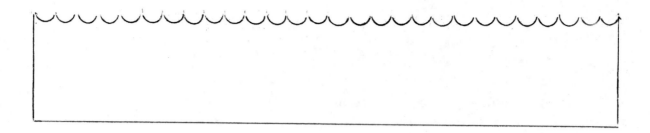

Fig. 12-1: Washboard Finish. (Exaggerated)

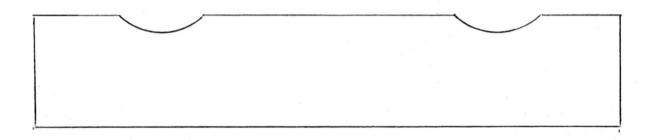

Fig. 12-2: Clip Marks. (Exaggerated)

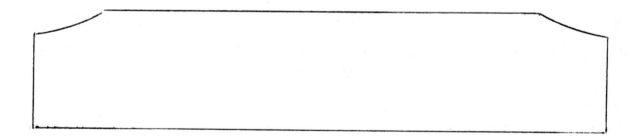

Fig. 12-3: Snipe. (Exaggerated)

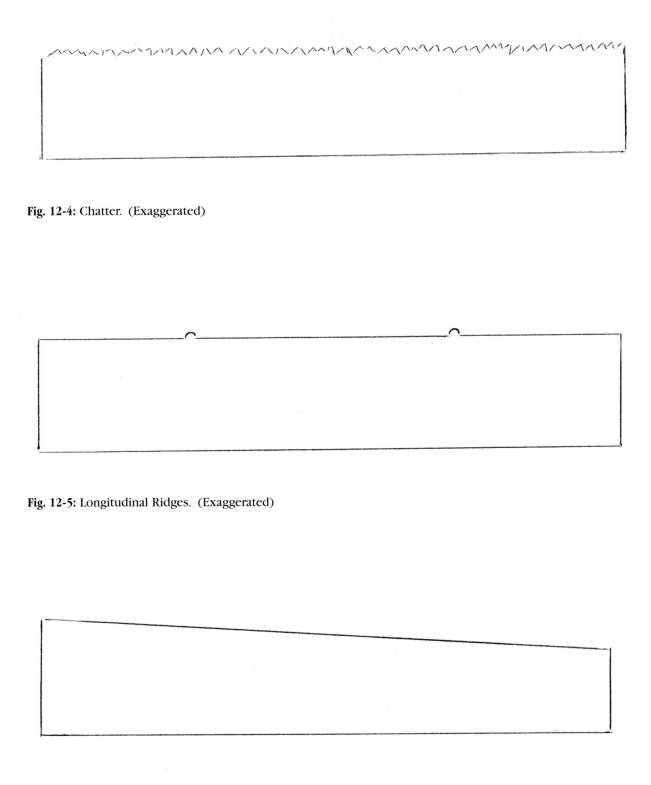

Fig. 12-4: Chatter. (Exaggerated)

Fig. 12-5: Longitudinal Ridges. (Exaggerated)

Fig. 12-6: Taper. (Exaggerated)

Chapter 13

PRACTICAL INFORMATION AND HELPFUL HINTS

INFLUENCE OF CUTTERHEAD SPEED & FEED ON FINISH

The use of high cutterhead speeds allows faster feed rates while still maintaining the same quality of planing. The faster a board is fed through, the farther it will travel between each cut, resulting in a coarser finish unless the cutterhead speed is increased as well. A low feed rate and light cuts tend to give a better finish.

A planed surface consists of microscopic waves at right angles to the direction of the feed. It is commonly assumed the number of knife marks per inch mainly defines the quality of a planed surface, the more knife marks per inch, the better the planing. Actually, it is not so much the closeness of the marks, but the height of the waves which determines quality. In general, machined surfaces are improved by maintaining low values for feed per knife and the height of knife marks—usually accomplished by increasing the cutting-circle diameter, the number of jointed knives in the cutterhead, and by reducing the feed speed.

The spacing or pitch (P) of these waves is mainly governed by three factors and can be calculated using the formula $P=NR/12F$: the speed of the cutterhead (R) in rpm, the feed speed (F) in fpm, and the number of knives (N). For example, a three knife cutterhead running at 3,500 rpm at a feed rate of 30 fpm: $P=(3 \times 3500)/(12 \times 30)=29$ marks per inch.

A four-knife cutterhead running at 3,450 rpm at 40 fpm will result in 28.8 knife cuts per inch; at 70 fpm, 16.4. While a twenty knife, 3,500 rpm, cutterhead at 200 fpm will give 28.8. There is a diminishing return after this point; an increase in speed leads to a decrease in finish.

The general grading standard is: under 8 marks per inch, poor; 8-12, general work; 12-18, interior work; and 18-25, high-class millwork and furniture.

Because motor speed (r) and cutterhead speed (R) vary inversely with the diameters of the motor pulley (d) and the cutterhead pulley (D), the pitch can be manipulated somewhat. $R=(d)/(D) \times (r)$. For example: a motor pulley 8" in diameter running at 3,500 rpm driving a cutterhead with a 4" pulley: $R=(8/4) \times 3,500=7,000$ rpm.

LIGHT CUTS ON SOFT MATERIAL

The finished surface of a softwood board with the cut set at 1/32" or less, may show marks put there by the corrugated infeed roll. This indicates there is too much spring pressure on the roll for such material and a light cut. A deeper cut would naturally remove the marks. This is corrected by relieving the spring pressure on the infeed roll but only the infeed roll. Leave the rest alone. Remember that the pressure screws must be turned the same number of revolutions. Though the gripping power of the roll has been reduced, light cuts require less.

The opposite is also true. Heavy cuts require heavy infeed roll pressure.

DETERMINING MINIMUM BOARD LENGTH

Lumber must be long enough to engage the outfeed rollers before it leaves the infeed rollers. The shortest lumber that you may plane must be at least 2" longer than the distance between the rolls in the bed, usually not less than 14". Measure the distance from the midsection of the infeed roll to the midsection of the outfeed roll.

HORSE POWER

Generally speaking if the machine is not over 24" in width, a 5-hp motor is ample; a light duty 16" or 18" planer requires about 3 hp. However, if your planer has Babbitt bearings, which create more friction than modern ball or tapered bearings and also lacks the means to allow the motor to come up to speed before engaging the cutterhead, a 24" may require a 7-hp motor and the 16" to 18" a 5-hp motor.

The new 5-hp, 220-volt, three-phase motor on my White 24 x 8 planer refused to start under load even with the feed disengaged. I solved my problem by tinkering together an idler pulley system. Once the motor was fully up to speed, I engaged the cutterhead and the planer ran perfectly.

If needed, you can calculate the approximate horsepower of an unknown single phase motor by multiplying the motor amperage by the voltage, dividing that sum by 746 (the number of watts required to produce one horsepower), and then taking 85% of the result to allow for friction losses.

CUTTERHEAD SPEED

The cutterhead normally operates at a fixed speed of about 3,600 rpm but 4,200-5,000 rpm is not uncommon. Cutterheads with Babbitt bearings should operate between 3,000 to 3,500 rpm.

FEED RATES

The feed should be varied with the width of lumber, the kind of wood, and the desired quality of finish. Fairly wide, hard wood should be fed at a relatively slow speed, and narrower pieces of softer wood at a higher feed. If the rate of feed is too fast for the cutterhead speed, the finish will be rough and show knife marks; if too slow, the cutting edge becomes worn due to the knife scraping instead of cutting. Variable speed rolls cannot be adjusted unless the rolls are turning.

LONG LUMBER

If a very heavy and long board is permitted to leave the planer unsupported, it may lift into the cutterhead slightly, clipping the end, unless the pressure bar is set very tightly. But this increases friction and causes feeding problems.

Once the infeed roller grips the lumber and begins pulling it past the cutterhead, move to the outfeed side of the machine. Support the work piece with both hands until it clears the outfeed roller. A slight, continuous lift on the end helps prevent snipe by keeping the board flat on the table. I've found it best to always support long overhanging lumber on both ends in a similar manner to prevent snipe.

SMOOTH FINISH

For an exceptionally smooth finish, feed slowly.

A planer, when set correctly, will usually deliver a better finish than the jointer, so it's a good idea to turn the board over, once the second face has been established, to plane the original face as well.

ROUGHING CUTS

For rough planing where surface quality is not as important, feed fast.

It is good practice to get close to the eventual thickness with heavy cuts then make the final pass with a light cut for a better finish.

CROSS-GRAINED LUMBER

Tear on cross-grained lumber can be minimized by deliberately feeding the lumber through the planer at an angle, much like making a skew cut on a jointer. However, you must make sure that the angled board can pass through the planer without striking the planer's table guides or frame.

Remember that if a long board should be started inadvertently in a diagonal direction or at too sharp an angle, a quick sidewise pull or push at the start will straighten it.

Often, the worst crossed grain in a board is located on one end. For safety, it is best to feed this end first so no piece can be torn out by the knives. If fed the other way, quite often a piece will be torn out and remain in the machine. The next board entering will push this tapering piece along and over the next roll where it can slip down and wedge itself into the small opening between the bed and roll. Most likely, the piece will have its top slightly above the bed, and every subsequent board will be marred its entire length. Removing the chip may require cranking down the bed and forcing the chip out by pushing from below with a narrow bladed tool.

REMOVING LARGE AMOUNT OF LUMBER

If a great deal of material must be removed from a board it is good practice to plane off an equal amount on both sides with alternating cuts. The board might warp or cup if the moisture content is not the same on both sides. The surface from which the larger amount of lumber is removed usually has the higher moisture content, because the center of a piece of wood generally contains more moisture than the surface. An exposed surface having a higher moisture content will dry out resulting in contraction producing a concave surface. The reverse may occur if the piece is exposed in a very moist atmosphere.

Actually, to help prevent lumber from warping, planing from both sides of any work piece rather than removing thickness from one side only is a good idea.

REDUCING SQUARE LUMBER TO SIZE

When reducing square lumber, such as posts or table legs, to size with a planer, two adjacent sides must first be squared on the jointer and these marked as working faces. When they are run through the planer, a working face should always be placed on the bed of the machine. Planing blocks that have been inadvertently cut or jointed at an angle will simply yield the same angles, only with a smooth finish.

THIN LUMBER

Ordinarily a planer will not handle lumber thinner than 1/4", though some are designed to handle as little as 1/16".

When it is necessary to plane lumber thinner than 5/16", great care should be taken to select lumber with the straightest grain possible. The thinner the lumber, the straighter the grain should be. It does not take a very deep tearing cut on such lumber to tear completely through at some point. Full thickness pieces will be torn out.

Precautions such as taking light cuts, putting the material through several times, or running the lumber slower, or both, can help. Modern planers are better at planing thin material than older models. Use of a backing board is recommended.

Reduce the lumber to 5/16" or 1/4" thickness in the usual manner. Then select a board 1" thick. This piece must be wider and longer than the thin lumber. Reduce the piece to a uniform thickness, not less than 3/4".

Create a ledge or stop on one end of the backing board by securely gluing a wooden strip across it slightly less than the thickness of the intended finished material. Another method is to glue and screw a cleat against the board's end that projects the proper height. This will keep the thin board from shooting off and prevents the knives from striking a screw point. Make light cuts. Mark the thickness of the backing board and keep it for future use. Eventually you'll have a comprehensive set of backing boards for different thicknesses.

BOWED OR CUPPED LUMBER

It is best to feed the lumber through with the cup on the table. Since it has a two-line contact with the rolls and the table it feeds with greater stability and less rocking. Lumber 1" or less will often split under the pressure of the rolls while passing through the machine. The crack always takes the direction of the grain.

Since the split section must be removed, there is a loss in width but not much in thickness. On lumber thick enough to withstand the pressure of the rolls and pressure bar without splitting, there is no width loss but a large thickness loss.

It is better to rip badly cupped lumber into narrower boards before running it through the planer. The narrow pieces still are slightly cupped but will plane flat with far less loss of thickness and trouble.

WIDE LUMBER & GLUE-UPS

After lumber has been glued up to make a large surface such as a tabletop, it is often too wide to have one face trued on a jointer first. In such cases, first remove as much dried glue as possible from the surfaces then set the feed at the slowest. Place the best surface (the smoothest) down, and make one light cut. Flip the piece over and make a cut on the other side at the same setting. Repeat the procedure using progressively heavier cuts until the board is smooth on both sides. Be sure to glue up the boards so that the grain runs in the same direction.

DEPTH OF CUT

Though production planers may remove 1/2" or more with a single pass, it's still not a good idea. Use common sense in setting the depth. It is easier on the machine to make several 1/16" or less cuts rather than a few 1/8" cuts.

To avoid overloading the machine, the depth of cut should be in proportion to the width of the material and the hardness. A planer will easily take a 1/16" cut on 8"-wide soft pine, while a similar cut on 20" pine would likely cause the machine to bog down. On 20" wide oak, a 1/32" cut would certainly slow down the machine maybe even stall it. As a rule, when planing wide lumber or hardwood, the cut should not be heavier than 1/32".

The amount of cut will be determined by the hardness or softness of the woods and the width of cut, and, to a certain extent, by the rate of feed. Too deep a cut will stall the machine, causing the feed belts to slip and the feed rolls to stop. In such

a case the machine has to be stopped and the depth of cut decreased, the feed being shut off until the cutterhead can come up to speed again.

A good operator learns to know by the sound of his machine when the load or feed is too heavy, and either throws off the feed promptly until the knives can pick up speed again, or, if the machine still stalls, decreases the cut slightly.

The final cut should leave the lumber slightly thicker than the specified size, say 1/64" to 1/32" to allow for sanding.

DETERMINING FIRST CUT

Lumber must be run through a planer successively until the proper thickness is obtained. If several pieces of similar thickness are to be surfaced, always measure for the thickest piece. Adjust the depth until the thickness-scale shows a setting 1/16" less than the thickest piece.

On a planer lacking a sectional infeed roll and chipbreaker where a number of pieces are to be planed, the thickest is planed first, the others being added in turn as soon as their thickness permits.

Rough sawn lumber can be tapered, sometimes severely. It is wise to check the lumber at different points along its length for variation in thickness and adjust the depth of cut accordingly. More so if you have a planer that has a short strip of metal fastened directly to the bottom of the top casting's front which acts as a limiting device to prevent too heavy of a cut. A tapered piece can easily wedge itself beneath this.

WARPED & TWISTED LUMBER

The chief function of a planer is to produce parallel surfaces by reducing lumber to uniform thickness. Contrary to popular belief, it will not straighten out lumber. That is the jointer's job. If a board enters the planer warped, it will leave it warped, though thinner. The pressure exerted by the feed rolls momentarily straightens the section of the board passing under the knives and holds it so while the wood is being removed.

However, just as soon as the pressure is relieved, the board springs back to its original shape.

A warped board must be straightened on a jointer first. True one face of the board on the jointer, and use this as the working face. The working face need not be perfectly flat but needs to have a level surface sufficient to support the board and keep it from rocking. Place the lumber on the bed with the working face down, and the grain turned so that the knives will cut with the grain.

STARTING LOAD

Release the feed mechanism by pulling back the lever or belt tightener controlling the feed rolls. This decreases the starting load. Start the machine and permit it to gain full speed, and then start the feed rolls by throwing the feed lever or belt tightener forward.

If the machine tends to choke or slow down, stop the feed until the machine regains its momentum. When the machine has regained full speed, engage the feed again.

MISCELLANEOUS HINTS

Run all the boards through on the last pass to ensure uniform thickness of all the pieces.

If the lumber varies in thickness, use the thickest part as a guide.

With a solid infeed roll it's better and safer to feed all the required lumber through the planer even if several pieces don't make contact with the knives at the first pass. This eliminates the annoyance of having some of the pieces get stuck later on because they are too thick. This means lowering the bed and losing your setting. After the first run or two, most of the boards should start to make contact with the knives and will cut smoothly.

Never plane varnished or painted lumber. Used lumber of any kind should never be run through a planer.

Feed each successive piece into the planer at a different location on the bed to avoid uneven wear on the knives, table, chipbreaker, and pressure bar. Likewise, do not do the entire cutting at one place when one board is being planed. Distribute it equally throughout the length of the knives so that they will wear down and dull evenly.

Chapter 14

ROUTINE MAINTENANCE

Regular inspection will ensure that the planer is in proper adjustment; that all screws, nuts, and bolts are tight; and that belts and chains are in good condition with proper tension. Buildup of sawdust and other debris can cause the planer to cut inaccurately so periodic cleaning is mandatory.

The cutterhead, feed rolls, table rolls, chipbreaker, and the table should be cleaned with a non-flammable solvent to remove pitch, gum, dirt, etc. It is foolish to adjust the table rolls to thousandths of an inch when they are caked with pitch and dirt perhaps 1/64" thick! Never use a sharp instrument to remove pitch or gum accumulation; a brush works best. Steel wool might be necessary in some cases. Remember the knives are like razors! Close-fitting parts such as the cutterhead slots and their gibs should be cleaned with a cloth or brush and solvent and freed from clinging foreign material.

The edge of the pressure bar which bears on the lumber also should be kept free of pitch accumulation and chips so as not to score the finished surface of the lumber.

All exposed cast-iron parts should be given a coat of paste wax as a lubricant and rust inhibitor. The wax will also decrease the buildup of dirt and dust. It's been my experience that waxing idler rolls tends to make them too slippery. Instead of rolling beneath the board they remain motionless and the board slides over them, bogging down the feed due to the friction.

It is difficult to establish a schedule as to how often a planer should be lubricated. Ordinarily it should be oiled and greased thoroughly every 24 hours of running time. Table roll bearings and feed roll bearings should be oiled every day or two if the planer is used continuously.

The recommended lubrication for roller chains is to simply wipe the chain clean though there are chain lubricants. When there is an appreciable build up of dust, dirt, or wood shavings, use an oil cloth. Drive chains should be lubricated every six months. Under severe applications lubricate the chains as required. Never pour oil directly on the chain. Over-oiling defeats the purpose of the lubrication, since it encourages the collecting of debris and works into the links. This speeds up wear and leads to premature replacement.

Gear box oil should be changed once a year. Gear boxes are sealed. There will be a drain plug at the chamber's bottom. Depending on the planer's size, the box may require several pints. The gear box should be filled to the oil level plug with SAE 140-W or SAE 600-W non-detergent motor oil. If the exact type of required lubrication is unknown, SAE 90-140-W gear box oil can generally be used. However, planers such as Yates-American's J-180 and Delta's 22-212 require SAE 600-W worm gear oil.

The feed work gears on American Saw Mill Machinery Co.'s 1931 Monarch planer all ran in lubricant in the base of the machine.

Oil-impregnated bronze bushings usually found on all roller bearing blocks should not require further lubrication.

Alemite-fitted ball bearings should be lubricated about twice a year with standard bearing grease.

Occasionally apply a thin oil over the top of the entire sectional roll. When the outer sections

.eir normal central position the
.eplacing.

..nber, oil goes in oil chambers and
_ in grease fittings. Check oil sight glasses
.riodically and add oil as needed.

On variable feed planers it's wise to run the motor up and down daily to keep a thin film of oil on the pulley roto-cone shaft, otherwise the cone pulley may freeze.

Periodically apply a few drops of light oil to the wedge ways, elevating screws, and variable speed pulley on the feed motor. Oil between gibs and column casting.

An exhaust system is recommended, particularly when a planer is used in production work and there is a sizable buildup of shavings.

Unless your planer shows a tendency to "walk" across the shop floor, do not fasten it down. Usually the sheer weight of a machine will keep it in place. Holes in bases were most often put there to bolt the machine to a shipping crate or pallet. Bolting the machine to an uneven floor can twist the frame or even break it. Be certain the base is evenly and firmly supported, using hardwood wedges if needed, so it will not distort when the bolts holding it to the floor are tightened.

AFTERWORD

In order to make any future editions of *The Planer Truth* even better, and perhaps larger and more detailed, the author welcomes all comments, criticisms (good or bad), suggestions, additions, and corrections from readers. Input from the experienced owners and operators of vintage planers, who are very knowledgeable about the various quirks of their individual machines, are much hoped for. There are plenty of the machines out there. The author is also anxious to obtain planer manuals, original or photocopies, old or new. With luck, the book could go from being a general guide on vintage planers to a definitive book on the subject.

Please write (don't call) to: Mr. Dana Martin Batory, 402 E. Bucyrus St., Crestline, OH 44827.

INDEX

American Saw Mill Machinery Co.
Jewel Planer 13, 17, 36
Monarch Planer 147
American Wood Working Machine Co.
No. 1 Surfacer 47
No. 4 1/2 Surface Planer 41
No. 5 Surfacer 90
Bentel & Margedant Co. 18
No. 41 Monitor Surface Planer 34
No. 42 Hamilton Surface Planer..........43
No. 44 Diagonal Surface Planer 18, 60
No. 52 Power Feed Planer 60-Inch 62
Boice-Crane Co. 69
Little Giant Planer 14, 29
Buss Machine Works
No. 208 Planer 20 x 8-Inch 10, 116, 119, 121,
124, 126, 135
Clement, Frank H. Co.
No. 1 Improved Planer And Smoother..........110
No. 3 Improved Double Belted Surfacer 113
Crescent Machine Co. 84
No. 218 Planer 15
No. P-18 Planer 112
No. P-24 Planer 66
Planer 26 x 8-Inch 67, 68
Variable Speed Planer 30 x 6-Inch 11, 23
Daniels Planer...................................1, 2, 9
Defiance Machine Work
Four Roll Surface Planer 26-Inch 69
Delta
No. 22-101 Planer 110, 118, 120, 122, 128
No. 22-212 Planer 110, 117, 120, 122
No. 22-401 Planer 110, 118, 120, 122
Farrar, James 14
Fay, J. A. & Co. 12
Granite State Improved Planing, Tongueing And Grooving
Machine 12
Yankee Cylinder Planing Machine 20, 68
Fay, J. A. & Egan Co.
No. 156 New Cabinet Smoothing Planer 70, 99
No. 19 Improved Extra Heavy Planer And Smoother 63, 70
Greenlee Brothers & Co.
No. 110 Six-Roll Planer 12, 14, 28, 57, 74, 77, 100
Helpful Hints
Cutterhead Speed 143
Depth of Cut 145
First Cut 145
Minimum Board Length 142
Feed Rates 143
Horse Power 143
Influence Of Cutterhead Speed & Feed On Finish 142
Light Cuts On Soft Material 142
Miscellaneous 146
Bowed or Cupped Lumber 144
Cross-Grained Lumber 143
Long Lumber 143
Thin Lumber 144
Warped and Twisted Lumber 145
Wide Lumber and Glue-Ups 145
Reducing Square Lumber To Size 144
Removing Large Amount Of Lumber 144
Roughing Cuts 143
Smooth Finish 143
Starting Load 146
Norris Improved Diagonal Planer 18

Northfield Foundry & Machine Co.
No. 5 Surfacer...............................68, 91
Oliver Machinery Co. 55
No. 299 Planer 33, 110, 117, 122, 123, 125
No. 361 Surface Planer 25
No. 61 Four-Roll Double Belted Surfacer 52, 86
Power, L. & Co. 27, 51, 107
Powermatic
No. 100 Planer 118, 125
No. 160 Planer 109, 125
No. 201 Planer 109, 125, 128
Powis, James & Co. 11
Richardson, Meriam & Co. 1, 5
No. 0 Small Cylinder Planing Machine 9
No. 2 Woodworth Planer 3, 16
Rogers, C. B. & Co.
No. 7 and No. 8 Planers 31, 32
Rowley & Hermance Co.
Peacemaker Double Belted Surfacer 36, 68
Smith, H. B. Machine Co.
New Surface Planing Machine 68, 88
No. 30-A Cabinet Surfacer 12, 29
Stetson-Ross Co. 1
Troubleshooting
Chain Jumping 139
Chatter 137
Chip Marks 138
Clip Marks 137
Crushed Corners 137
Fuzzy, Rough, or Raised Grain 139
Halted Feeding 136
Longitudinal Ridges 138
Rounded or Glossy Surface 139
Snipes.......................................137
Stalled Lumber 136
Taper 138
Torn Grain 139
Twisting 138
Washboard Finish 137
White, John A. Co.
Planer 24 x 8-Inch 10
Whitney, Baxter D. 12-17, 26, 32
Whitney, Baxter D. & Son Co.
No. 29 Surfacer 37
No. 32 Surfacer 38, 68
No. 37 Heavy Duty Planer 81
Whitney, Baxter D. Co.
Silver Medal Planer..........................13, 37
Williamsport Machine Co.
New And Improved Surface Planer 68, 90
No. 3 Surfacer 68
Wilson, Henry 11
Woodbury, J. P. 71
Woods, S. A. Machine Co. 8, 11, 15-18
Improved Door Planer 18, 59
Woodworth Planer 2, 12
Yates, P. B. Machine Co.
No. 151 Surfacer 61
No. 156 Cabinet Planer 68, 92
No. 5 Planer 68
Yates-American Machine Co.
B-4 Direct Motor Driven Surfacer 66
J-180 Planer 122